ROOTS
&
BRANCHES

AN EXCITING COLLECTION OF GENEALOGICAL SUCCESS STORIES

ROOTS
&
BRANCHES

AN EXCITING COLLECTION OF GENEALOGICAL SUCCESS STORIES

CONNIE RECTOR AND DIANE DEPUTY

ISBN: 0-934126-78-X

First Printing, July 1985

Randall Book Co.
Salt Lake City, Utah

Lithographed in the United States of America

Typography by Executype
Salt Lake City, Utah

Table of Contents

Preface

Some people seem to look at life in a temporal way, caring only about the needs of the hour and provisions for this day. They speak of fun and food, fads and fashions, apparently having long given up anything of eternal value. Many others, however, are possessed by a yearning to know if there is a purpose to life, a more meaningful existence. Thoughts like: "Who am I?" "Does anyone really care about me?" "Why does my life seem empty?" "Who can help me?" "Is there a God?" "Where did I come from?" "Is this life all?" are questions that cause reflection. As an old Hebrew proverb says, "There must be a stirring below before there is a stirring above."

Some of the contributors to this collection had such questions in their earlier years which they share with us, then tell their solutions. Others found answers through more than coincidental happenings. The Old Testament seer Malachi prophesied:

> "Behold, I will send you Elijah the prophet before the great and dreadful day of the Lord: And he shall turn the heart of the fathers to the children, and the heart of the children to their fathers, lest I come and smite the earth with a curse" (Malachi 4:5-6).

Surely the Spirit of the Lord and the Spirit of Elijah is striving with us and our contemporaries.

These stories reaffirm our own experience that first we must establish our own identity. Once we know who we are, then there is the kindred question, "To what larger family do I belong?" This question has universal application for so few know with any assurety the depth, breadth and height of their own heritage.

There is great variety in the way our authors have gone about the task of preserving their heritage, and uniting the living with their dead through many generations. Their problems, puzzles, procedures and prayers are revealed to us in these personal accounts. All of the modern methods of gathering have been employed, together with God's eternal privileges of inspiration, revelation and other spiritual gifts.

We, as the compilers, have been thrilled by the accounts of these who have generously shared their inspiring stories. We believe they will provide inspiration and motivation to help others understand their own identity. Increased love and understanding among immediate and extended family members often follows the gathering of family history. Genealogy also teaches appreciation for different cultures and acceptance of all kinds of people. These varied experiences answer in one way or another the questions which are vital to all humans: "Is there a creator?" "Does He hear our prayers?" "Does life have real purpose?" "Does life continue after death?" "Is this life a pattern for the next?" "Will we ever be reunited with loved ones?"

Job, the Old Testament prophet, wrote:

> "For enquire, I pray thee, of the former age, and prepare thyself to the search of their fathers:
> (For we are but of yesterday, and know nothing, because our days upon earth are a shadow:)
> Shall not they teach thee, and tell thee, and utter words out of their heart?" (Job 8:8-10).

Job's testimony is recorded: "For I know that my redeemer liveth, and that he shall stand at the latter day upon the earth: And though after my skin worms destroy his body, yet in my flesh shall I see God:" (Job 19:25-26).

Like Job we "enquire of . . . former ages and prepare to . . . search of . . . fathers." As we ponder these scriptures, we marvel at Job's understanding and testimony and realize that he was a keeper of vital historical records.

Roots and Branches is also a historical record, a collection of some of the experiences of twentieth century seekers written by the searchers themselves. They reveal insights into many facets of life of more recent centuries which makes for interesting reading. We are grateful for the generosity with which these authors share their tales. Perhaps genealogists, like other historians, love a good story.

Connie Rector & Diane Deputy

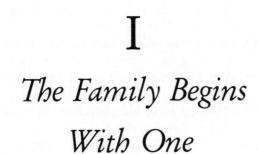

I

The Family Begins
With One

PATRICIA DUNSON SMITH

THE ARAPAHO KID

By Patricia Dunson Smith

I had worked intently at the IGI Microfiche for a considerable time, and becoming weary, I looked up for the first time and noticed a young Indian boy sitting across from me. Something said to me, "Get up and go talk to him," but he was very scruffy and even across the wide library table it was evident that he was in need of a good scrubbing. No way was I going to talk to him. I kept my eyes on the Manitoba records in front of me. Again, something said, "Get up and go talk to him." This is crazy, I thought. What would I say to a stranger? The third time, a more urgent feeling came over me, "Get up and go talk to him!" Reluctantly, I got up, went around to the other side of the table, leaned over the boy's shoulder, and said, "What tribe are you from?" Looking up at me he answered, "My dad's part-Arapaho and my mom's folks are some sort of Indians from the Northwest tribes." Looking me over he asked, "What tribe are you from?" I replied that some of my family were Sioux and others were Quinealt Taholahs. The boy's eyes got real wide, "I was up fishin' last summer on the Quinealt reservation. I stayed with some Pickernells." I gasped and had to steady myself against the edge of the table. "You mean," I said, "some of Aunt Bessie Pickernell's family?" "Yep," he replied. "She's sort of my distant relative."

We moved to an unoccupied table. I knew he *had* to be kin to me. He showed me his "U.S. Indian blue card" which every Indian must carry. It stated that his name was Mike Boxer, he was 16 years old, and he was listed as Arapaho. He repeated that his mother was from the Northwest tribes, but he had little knowledge about her lineage or her "whereabouts." He had been drifting from place to place and was now living with a young female who was a relative. She had allowed him to stay if he would babysit her children at night while she worked.

I saw that Mike had come to the library without a pencil or paper. "Why are you here?" I asked. The boy's eyes looked far away. "I wanted to know who I was." I choked back the tears. "Mike, come with me." I led him to the book stacks where my Laframboise family book was shelved. Taking it down, I showed Mike some of his mother's families. Mike was my second cousin! I told him about the great chiefs from whom he'd descended. As-Kal-Wish, Comcomley and Light House Charley. We photocopied the pertinent material from my book and also items from a book called *Rolls of Certain Indian Tribes of Washington and Oregon*, by McChessney.

When I handed Mike the records, I knew why I had been prompted to speak to him. As he left the library I extended my hand to say goodbye. Instead, he grabbed me in a big bear hug, pounded me soundly on the back and gave me a son's loving kiss on the cheek. I was very ashamed of my first response toward this Arapaho kid. Now I overlooked his appearance and saw him as a lonely young man searching for some meaning in his life, grasping for roots to hold onto. I watched him as he went toward the door, clutching many pages of his family history. Was it my imagination or did he square his shoulders and walk taller? "Farewell, Borraqui," (my friend) I said softly.

MORE PRESSING MATTERS

By Elizabeth C. Wyant Faul

I have in my possession copies of several letters written shortly after 1800 by my second great-grandfather, John Cheyney, to his brother, William, back in Chester County, Pennsylvania. He ended one letter with the sentence, "May the Director of the Universe direct you all safe to happiness." It is easy to deduce from this sentence that they were a good people with charitable thoughts toward one another. The father of John was Squire Thomas Cheyney who warned George Washington that the British were nearly upon them, when they were situated on the Brandywine. Thomas was called the "Paul Revere of Pennsylvania," an appellation I would never have known if not for genealogy!

I enjoyed history, even as a child. Today I love to glean my people's histories from whatever book, film or file I may find them.

Two or three years after starting my genealogical research, I became very discouraged about work on the line of my maternal grandmother, Laura Miranda Smith, who married William Cheyney, grandson of the above John. (It seems that in every generation of Cheyney families the names William and John are repeated over and over again.)

Anyway, the difficulty on the Smith line lay in the fact that I could not find the names of her brothers and sisters. Mother could only remember nicknames, and Grandmother had already passed on. At that time I operated a tiny dry-cleaning, press and alteration shop in Long Beach. Working ten and twelve hour days did not leave much time for such activities as reading census films. There was no possible way I could do research in any library, so I hired a genealogist. The cost was prohibitive, however, and I knew that when that research was finished, I would have to be on my own. I had to put Grandmother Laura Cheney's line aside for the time being.

Sometime later, I was standing at the counter in my shop when the mailman stepped in. Among the mail was a small pamphlet published in Long Beach called *The Searcher*. I started leafing through it back to front (as usual), when two names in the queries section caught my eye: "Laura M. Smith married William Cheyney." I read on. It gave the names of Laura's parents and her brothers and sisters! There they were—there was no mistaking the names of my grandparents!

I've always been grateful that there were no customers in the shop at that time. Between laughing, crying and giving thanks, I guess I must have sounded hysterical! After closing the shop that evening, I sat down and wrote to the person who had inserted that ad. I told her that I had no information to exchange, but how grateful I was that she had placed the ad in *The Searcher*. I explained that I was a granddaughter of Laura M. Smith Cheyney and that I had given up working on that line because I did not have any names to work with. She responded immediately, and it turned out that our great-grandfathers were brothers. Within a week she sent me direct-line marriages on the Smiths clear back to England to the year 1597! I was able to help her in a small way after all. She requested the names of all the descendants of my grandmother. I was more than happy to supply her with the names and information I had.

The experience, which provided information on the Smith/ Cheyney lines, came about through "natural" means, one might say, but this next experience, again using genealogical ads and queries, demonstrates how we can be prompted by the Spirit. I believe that all of us, at some time or another, have had an inexplicable "feeling" for someone or something. I had such a feeling for an ad in the *Genealogical Helper Exchange Issue*. I don't remember the year of the edition, but I do remember the number of the ad: "F1 submitted by Mrs. Merlin Faas of North English, Iowa." Several names and places mentioned in that ad gave me an extraordinary feeling that I was completely encircled but untouched. I read the ad several times and could not even find a hint that any of the names could belong to my line, but for some reason I kept going back to it. I finally made up my mind to do something about it.

Mrs. Faas lived in an area close to where my second great-grandparents, Samuel and Eliza Jane (McCombs) Wyant, had lived. I had not been able to locate their place of burial. So I sat down and wrote to Mrs. Faas. I told her how her ad in the *Helper* had caught my attention until I felt I had to do something about it. I apologized for sounding like a foolish old woman, and I asked if she knew of any old burial grounds which might possibly be the final resting place of my second great-grandfather, Samuel Wyant.

Within a few short days, I received a three-page, singlespaced, typewritten letter from Mrs. Faas giving me names and addresses of distant relatives of mine, plus the name and location of the White Pigeon Cemetery where my second great-grandparents and many other distant relatives were interred. I couldn't believe it!

A few years ago on the way to visit my mother in Nebraska, my daughter and I made a fast trip to my father's hometown. We arrived in Eagleville, Missouri about 2:30 that afternoon, hot and thirsty. When we saw a little sundries store, we stopped and went inside. Soon a tall, thin old gentleman was serving us frosty orange drinks.

They were so refreshing! I told him who I was and asked if he could put us in touch with some of our Wyant cousins. He could and did. "Helen Cooke lives only a couple of blocks away," he said. We went over immediately, introduced ourselves and explained why we were there. Then we asked her if she could help us with any family information. Our cousin graciously invited us in. I couldn't have been more than a couple of steps inside the door when she handed me a sheaf of papers. (They must have been very handy.) While I sat down and shuffled through them, Helen phoned someone by the name of "Elfie" who apparently lived a couple of miles out of town. She was there in a matter of minutes, and we had a terrific "family tree fest"!

Elfie persuaded us to stay overnight with her, and later she handed me two different bundles of papers! The first was a personal history of the oldest son of the ancestor of her branch of the family, namely Aaron Wyant, a younger brother of my Samuel Wyant. The second batch of papers consisted of all the descendants of Aaron, organized into family groups!

It seemed everyone I met was willing to share, and we were deeply grateful to get the records. As Elfie handed me the papers, she remarked that she had often wondered why she didn't just throw those papers away after she had copied them! Now I knew why for several months I had felt I had to make this trip into Missouri.

These experiences and others that have happened to me since I started genealogical work have convinced me that this is indeed the work of the Lord. It seems I have always had a deep-seated desire to learn about my people, and I am deeply grateful for the purpose and direction this work has given to my life.

BLESSED BEYOND BELIEF

By John W. Johnson

Several years ago I had the misfortune to lose my right leg in an accident, and I was sure that my future had just passed. My wife, Beulah, persuaded me to try doing some genealogy as a hobby to help pass the time and take my mind off my problems.

I could not carry books and walk with my crutches, so she went to the archives with me and carried the books that I needed. She helped me so much in the way of research—and self-esteem.

During the year that I was on crutches I typed genealogical records for others. I discovered that seven families whose records I typed had ancestors common with my lines! I used the money that I earned to pay my church budget and building fund. It helped me pay my "debt to the Lord." Of course, I found that I could not really repay Him because He continued to pour out blessings. My wife and I have been blessed so that I had my own business, from which I am now retired and living in a home that I designed.

Last winter, just before Beulah and I celebrated our fiftieth wedding anniversary, I developed serious heart problems. The doctor said I would not withstand surgery, so now I'm home on oxygen and restricted to a 50-foot cord. For a time I was so weak and shaky I could hardly sign a check. But I'm doing better each day. I bought a computer, and I'm enjoying that. I can't waste my time being discouraged—there is too much work to be done!

Through the years I have researched and collected between 1,000 and 1,500 family group sheets. Now I'm reviewing all my records and entering them into the computer. What used to take me an hour by hand can now be accomplished in seconds. I can quickly print out copies to send to relatives. It's so easy! I have encouraged between thirty-five to forty people to do their genealogy by computer. Now they can easily see the flow of their ancestors—who's who and where they belong on the family tree. (These days, if something comes out of a box, it makes more sense to people.)

In genealogy work one needs to be able to imagine how and when a person lived and in what time period. One family might have been happy with a dirt floor in a log cabin while another would have been used to a life of riches. To understand what your ancestors were like is to understand more about yourself.

I have been blessed beyond belief for my work in genealogy. You know, it's great to find out we're related to a famous king or queen, but we need to remember that we're related to horse thieves and bank robbers, too! Everyone has problems, but everyone's life is interesting. If we could understand we're all related to one another, maybe there wouldn't be wars because we wouldn't want to be fighting our own brothers.

When I finish my family group sheets and pedigree charts, I will begin writing family histories—right back to the beginning—if the Lord continues to spare my life.

A FUTURE HOMEMAKER FOR AMERICA

By Michele Bonilla "Lillie"

Most people have only one family, but I have two; the family in which I was born and my foster family! When I was young, all the children in my class worked on family trees. The teacher gave each of us a form to fill out. Because I was living in a foster home, I added the names of my foster family. At that time I didn't know much about my birth-family, but I do now.

I enjoy being a student at Bingham High School and try very hard to get good grades. Last year as a freshman, I enjoyed running cross-country. This year I am really involved in the Future Homemakers of America. Our major goal is to build good homes for America's future. As we study to become good homemakers, we learn many useful skills. One of my goals this year has been to improve my cooking, so I have been taking a home-ec class, saving recipes and doing more cooking at home for the family. In F.H.A. we look forward to the time when we can have happy families of our own.

In January a special friend of mine had a dream about me and how I love to bake. We were mixing a *huge* cake to serve many people. The cake represented my genealogy. How great it could be to gather the records of my ancestors and share them with my other relatives. We needed some money to help pay for the project but not too much. We were so happy and excited about our super project. I realized that genealogy is much greater than I ever thought it would be, interesting and not too difficult. My friend wrote her dream and gave me a copy to keep.

Last February, for one of our F.H.A. club projects, we were in charge of the Valentine's Day festivities for Sweetheart's Week. In order to qualify for the Sweetheart's Queen, we were judged on baking a cake, wearing a formal gown, and being able to answer questions about F.H.A.

I thought about my cake for several days. I wanted it to be different and special. On Saturday, while I was mixing and baking my cake, I was thinking about how I would decorate it. When I finally opened the oven door, the fragrant lemon smell was wonderful! I laid the two heart-shaed layers on a cake board to cool, and placed them side-by-side like a twin valentine. I iced them with vanilla frosting, then decorated the shell borders and lettering in red. The inscription read, "Home Is Where The Heart Is." As the finishing touch, I put a little brown frosted house by the word "Home," and a red heart after the words "Heart Is." It looked really pretty. I was chosen to be second attendant to the queen, and I had a wonderful time!

I let my interest in genealogy slump for a while, but now that I am fifteen years old, I have started finding new and interesting things about my families.

My foster parents, Ralph and Emily Lillie, have been good examples in my life. I am very happy in this family for we try hard to accomplish many fun things that we have set out to do. They support me in F.H.A. and other school activities. We work together in the garden and on many different projects that must be done. They help me fulfill my short and long-term goals. I have enjoyed the other foster children that have come and gone through the years.

MICHELE BONILLA "LILLIE"

My foster mom has told me much about the history of our family. Records have been kept and much genealogy has been done. Mom's family came from Denmark and Sweden; Dad's from England. Grandma has a large family history book. We enjoy reading about the families and attending reunions. Mom has encouraged me to find out more about my birth family.

When I visit my birth parents, Frank and Margaret Bonilla, we sometimes talk about our family history. I learned that my father's parents sailed from Europe to San Francisco, then were sent to the Hawaiian Islands where they lived for many years. Some of my relatives live there today.

My birth-mother's family also originated in Europe, but many years ago. She has helped me find much new information. I have learned many things about her background from reading old letters and books that belonged to my great-aunt. One day while working at my friend's home, it took me twice as long to finish because I was exchanging family information on the phone! The next day one of our Sunday School teachers was ill, and I was invited to take her place and share all my research experiences. It was really exciting and so much fun!

I appreciated my friend's dream about mixing the huge genealogy cake because I often dream. One night I dreamed that my friend, Jeanene Bateman, and I were sitting in my Spanish class. Jeanene had brought her lunch to class which was very unusual. I had brought Italian dressing to add a little spice to her salad. While we were sitting together at a class table, I spilled the dressing, and it ran all over the table. I tried putting the dressing back in the bottle but couldn't. I remember telling Jeanene that I couldn't put it back. Then I woke up.

At first I thought it was just an ordinary dream, but later I thought that maybe it wasn't. I felt that this dream had something to do with my family history, so I call my birth-father to ask him where his mother was born. He answered, "She came from Barcelona, Spain." That evening I learned that many of my ancestors were Spanish. I wonder, if the Indian dressing, some of them had not "spilled over" from Italy. It will be exciting to find that out one day. I have encouraged Jeanen to start working on her own genealogy.

I strongly believe it is important to learn about your family background. I am finish my second year of Spanish, saving my money and looking forward happily to a trip to Spain.

ALL MY CHILDREN
By Karl-Michael Sala

In my work as an accredited genealogist, I feel a particular responsibility to find documented proof of *every* individual regardless of the circumstances surrounding his birth, life or death. Although some of my patrons are afraid of finding "skeletons in the closet," in one case, obtaining *all* the birth entries of a family was the key to unlocking the maternal ancestry. The mother's parish of origin was mentioned only in the birth of the illegitimate child and not in the parent's marriage entry or the birth of the other children. Some genealogists, clerks or clergymen do not tell their clients or correspondents about such cases, or they simply do not search in those years of life that may produce such information. A few of my clients have requested only the direct ancestral lineage *without* the children. One parish of origin was not found until the birth entry of the seventh child! I have found that it is important to research the *complete* family.

In a recent tough assignment I was given a case in Lippe (Detmold), West Germany. The Dreier family in Germany owned a large Stammbaum (detailed lineage chart) compiled years ago by a descendant living in the ancestral area. The information ended abruptly in the mid 1700s. The line was reported by the family and other researchers to have dead-ended temporarily. An area search was advised—a process of searching surrounding parishes with the hope of locating the ancestor not found in the target parish. In addition, the client asked me to make certain that *all* the children of every generation had been located for she felt, in spite of previous research, that there might be a possible omission. Of course, I was then to continue this "dead-ended" genealogy. I was to "follow the promptings from on High," as well as to use my expertise in Germanic research. Oh great, I thought. When I was being tested for German accreditation, I was not asked if I used God as a source. I had supposed the inspiration would come naturally—based on logic. I mean, if He wanted me to find something, He would give it to me. Right?

After analyzing the lineage and family charts of this client, I began "research as usual." I obtained detailed Prussian military maps of the area to determine the exact location of the towns and parishes. On the latest Dreier family sheet I rechecked the births of all listed children including the gaps of more than one year, several years before the first child and after the last. Although the first child, Herman Heinrich, was illegitimate, something prompted me to "look a little further." (Normally, one would assume this to be *the* one and only illegitimate child born to a couple.) Logically, I felt that further searching would be a waste of the client's research dollar. Logic also reminded me that I was charging on a project basis rather than an hourly fee, so it was my prerogative to continue. Indeed, I did find *another* illegitimate child born earlier, Friederike Wilhelmine! Whew!

On the next generation back of the same ancestral line, in the family of Hans Henrich Dreier and Anna Maria Ilsebein Pankuken, family births were again pursued. An additional child, Johann Friedrich Adolph, was born just a few months *after* the parental marriage. (The lesson here is to look for a legitimate birth *just* after a marriage as well as for prior illegitimacies.)

Going back one more generation to Johann Christoph Dreier and Anna Margareta Elisabeth Burkamps, I found *two additional* children, Johann Friedrich and Adolph Henrich Christophel, making a total of four. The latter two were born to the same father, but apparently to different mothers! Yet, the entries show that they were both legitimate births. Unbelievably, on the third entry, even though the two given names were identical, the mother's surname was the same as a *witness* on the previous birth, Greta Lisabeth Spilkers. However, no marriage record was located for this new "wife." Then as I found the birth of the fourth and last child, Adolph Henrich Christophel, the mother was again listed as having the same surname, Burkamps, as the mother of the first two children! Boy, am I ever sorry I took on this project, I thought. No, these things must be dealt with and ferreted out as much as possible, I thought further. In order to leave no stone unturned, I needed to apply concentrated effort on this line, whether or not I was successful. Time to recheck the map!

As I studied the detailed photocopies of the old maps, I realized that, unlike most German parishes I had researched, the pastor of Schötmar was responsible for a larger number of villages and towns. How could he and/or his staff possibly keep up with this huge number of parishioners? Well, apparently they didn't! A simple error must have been made. I concluded that, in spite of conflicting evidence, these four children were most likely born to the *same* parents. (Especially when I later found the death record of the father and his widow's name was listed as Burkamps, the same as the mother of the first, second and fourth child.)

Now I was back to the earliest known ancestor on the chart, Johann Christoph Dreyer. In order to properly identify him I searched the marriage records, but he was not there. Assuming he died in Schötmar parish where his family lived, I sought and found his death entry in 1775. It listed him as 50 years old, but no month or day was listed as in most of the entries. From this I calculated a year of birth which, of course, could have been approximate. Double checking, I could not find a 1725 birth under the known surname. Instead, I found three children born prior to that date to *probable* parents, Hans Hermann Dreier and Anna Ilsabey Albrings, who seemed to be the only possible family of that surname. (The couple was already married by that date, so Johann Christoph should not have been illegitimate.) By this time I was tired, so I put my head down and closed my eyes and decided I needed help! All records indicated that Johann Christoph should have been born in this parish but apparently was not. Perhaps I needed to try some creative research. As long as my eyes were closed, I thought I might as well say a little prayer.

Refreshed, I continued on with my work. Within ten minutes I found Johann Christoph, born *1728* with his father's name listed as Hans Hermann *Mejer,* a *different, sound-alike* surname. The *mother's* name, Anna Ilsabey Albrings, was the *same* as that in the birth entries of his siblings! Also, the marriage records showed no other man named Mejer marrying a woman named Albrings. In addition, one of the *witnesses* was named Christoph Mejer, so it was probably another misstatement. The residence mentioned on the entry, "Bey Albring zu Aspe" was the same as in the other sibling birth entries. Later, further support for my research hypothesis was found in the death entry of one of the siblings, Hans Henrich. He was recorded in the birth entry with the family surname, Dreyer, but when he died a quarter year later, he was listed as Hans Henrich Mejer!

Then, to complicate matters even more, I finally located the marriage record of the couple only to find that the name of the groom was listed Johan (Hans) Henrich Dreyman which bore a -man suffix rather than -er, but the residence, "auf Knolmans Hoff" also appeared in the witness column of some of the sibling birth entries. I did not find other Dreymans having children in the parish. Again, the wife's name, Anna Ilsabein Albrings/Alberdings, was the same as the mother of the children, so I knew I had finally found the right couple! Thus, I had extended the dead-ended line one more generation!

It was good to have a client who reminded me that logic and inspiration make good partners. (A substantial discount was provided to show my appreciation.)

Now, I suppose we could imagine a very grateful ancestor saying to us, "Thank you! You have found *all* my children!"

DESIGN FOR LIVING

By Helen Haggstrom King

It seems that every person adds his own color and design to the tapestry of life. Many choose vibrant values, bright and cheerful.

Others prefer soft tones of floss or fabric textures, muted and mellow, and some, the gray and somber materials. A few do not choose at all but are content with the remnants and ravelings of others.

My mother, Astrid Carlson Haggstrom, is a woman who created her own special family design. Since my father, Arthur H. Haggstrom, was seldom home, my devoted mother raised my brothers, Bob and Ted and I, herself. We were very close. On our weekly jaunts to the public library, she would check out stacks of books for us. She taught us to appreciate all kinds of art and classical music. I do believe my father was very proud of his children.

During my formative years I was lucky to have a mother who understood that I was different and encouraged me in those differences. She was a wonderful cook and dressmaker who taught me as a child to cook, sew, design my own clothes and keep a nice home.

All through school I took many art classes. Though I was a social person, I spent many nights drawing instead of dating. One high school teacher, Miss Robison, taught costume design. I loved it! In my tenth grade summer school, I attended Frank Wiggins Trade School in Los Angeles which pointed the way to my future profession.

After graduation I went back to Wiggins and studied design for almost four years. I had a wonderful time and painted over a hundred historical-costume plates. (I have given many of these as gifts. I also have an extraordinary collection of costume books and prints, all originals, dating back almost 200 years which I have used in design and which my daughter is now beginning to use for the same purpose.)

Then, Mother had a massive heart attack. I attended night school and cared for her during the day. My brothers took over while I was in school. We all worked together to help one another, and she pulled through quite nicely.

When I left trade school, I got a job with Emgee Novelty, designing trims for the wholesale garment trade. It was a very interesting business. We created decorations for shoes, handbags and hats, pants, blouses and dresses and evening wear. One of our enjoyable projects was designing the bathing suit trims for the Miss Universe beauty contest three or four years in a row. I worked and saved all my money so I could go to Europe and in particular to Paris.

I flew to New York and sailed to Europe. I applied for work in the fashion business in Paris, but was told the industry was still in the process of "gearing up" after the war. There was no possibility of employment. Nevertheless, with letters of introduction from New York, I was able to get to most of the big fashion houses and see many of their high-fashion shows. It was even more interesting to go backstage and see how things were really run.

During this time I took the opportunity to visit Holland, England, Switzerland and Italy. I lived in Paris, studied French and traveled all over France. I made friends everywhere I went. In Europe I found a different way of thinking about life. There, business was only a way to make a living, not an end in itself as so many Americans thought at that time. It gave me a lot to consider.

I returned to America, went back to my old job and enrolled at Otis Art Institute. For two years I studied painting, drawing and sculpture. I also enjoyed classes in ceramics, leatherwork and other media.

In 1958 I met Robert King, another artist, at a friend's coffee house. We were married within a month. He had been a seaman for many years, and when he left the sea, he became an artist. Bob said that one of us would have to work and the other create. So, I stayed home and created. Whatever I wanted to try, Bob bought the tools and materials for me. Our motto became, "If you *can't* make it, buy it!" I made everything, even my own dishes, and Bob made all the furniture.

Bob had lost track of his family through the years, so after we were married, we set out to trace his mother. We did not find her, however, until we had a son, Arthur, and a daughter, Valerie. She was a very surprised lady! She had remarried a proficient one-handed key-maker named Jack Chandler (who became Grandpa Jack). We really began to gather the family in. My mother and brothers were pleased.

Bob and I had a good life for a numbers of years until alcohol came into the picture. Bob always drank some, but it got worse. Though at home with my children, I began to make a life of my own. Bob's mother sent some raw turquoise to me, and it lay around the house for a couple of years. One day Bob suggested I take some classes to see whether I liked making jewelry. I soon found my forte as I loved creating jewelry from the raw stones and designing the metal framework to enhance the beauty of the gems. Each piece is unique. My God-given talent had finally found where it belonged!

In 1979 I regretfully said goodbye to my marriage. Alcohol had taken its toll. My children asked why I hadn't done this before. All my family and friends were supportive. I was able to retain our house and the art collection and start a new life.

I found a good job in a local department store doing credit and collection work. In addition, I have shown my jewelry in galleries and sold a number of pieces to private patrons. My jewelry is finally being recognized, and I hope to make a living creating jewelry from now on.

In February 1984 I visited my friend in Utah, and she took me to visit the points of interest including the library where I became interested in genealogy. The Scandinavian consultant, Ruth Manness, was very pleasant and helpful when I told her about my father, Arthur Haggstrom, born in January 1896 in Boden, Norbotten, Sweden. His father, Edward Haggstrom, emigrated to America in the early 1890s. (We later found the family in the 1900 Census of Nebraska.) It was a quiet day so Ruth searched while I ran back and forth finding and replacing films. Ruth mentioned that she would phone a Swedish lady who was working on Haggstrom research. We continued checking the films until lunchtime.

We were in the cafeteria when we saw the consultant bringing a lady to meet us. "This is Britt Lund, the Haggstrom lady I told you about," she explained. As we chatted, we discovered our families came from the same area in northern Sweden. When we returned to work, we had an ally to help us. In a short time we had traced the line back to Isak Aron Haggstrom from Svartbacken. We worked a couple of days and found *three* generations of my father's family. Isak Aron, born 1828, was the son of Johann Haggstrom, born 1783, a soldier of Skatamark!

It was exciting! I had never thought of families in this way before. They were always something everyone had, but so what? It's become very interesting to see a line when you chart it and can see where the family members came from and what they did for a living.

Later in the year I went back to Utah for another visit and did some more work with the same lady. We were able to get two more families back to 1745. We found the children of Johann Haggstrom, then searched for his father. When we found Jacob Johansen Fritzboege, we learned that Johann had changed his name to Haggstrom due to his area of service as a soldier. When I returned home, my family, especially my children were very pleased and interested in all I found.

In trying to find my mother's line, I was at a complete standstill until I learned that my Grandfather Carlson had come to the United States in the 1890s and changed his name. He returned to Sweden with a bride and a new name. That's where my next research will begin. I know as I do more genealogy, I will be in for many surprises!

Mother is still with us today and is an inspiration! I am building on her design as well as creating my own. I enjoy looking back to the patterns of the past—and forward to the future—as my children create their own unique designs for living.

FAITHFUL SON

By Eugene Ralph Fitzgerald

Now, may I write about myself, Eugene Ralph Fitzgerald. I was born in the month of January, 1944, on the 30th day. It was a wintry day. The family doctor helped my angel mother, Ruth Scott Fitzgerald, to give birth to me. I had yellow jaundice, and I believe this triggered something that made me a Mongoloid. Heavenly Father knew this.

My father, Victor Melville Fitzgerald, was a hard woker until he became ill and was in the hospital. He had several nervous breakdowns while I was small, so I didn't get to know him as well as I would have liked to. When he was well and able to be home with my mom and me, he would tell me stories about wild horses and Indians that I really enjoyed. I could picture them in my mind.

I was the youngest of six children: Ferris, Helen, LaDawn, Edna, Scott and I. We were raised on a beautiful farm. My Grandma Scott lived on a farm only two houses away. I enjoyed going there to have a slice of her homemade bread, spread thick with homemade butter and delicious jam. Sometimes I helped her make butter.

We had a fruit orchard. Sometimes I would climb the fruit trees and throw the fruit into my mother's apron. She taught me how to bottle fruit. She would say, "Son, I'm sure busy with the fruit," and ask me to help. She showed me how to peel the skins off peaches and take the pits out of apricots. I could make the sugar-water too and pour it in the jars. Then she would say, "That's fine. You're doing just fine!" (Later in school, I won a first place blue ribbon for my peaches and apricots.) I liked to help my mother. While she did the dishes, I dried and put them away in the cupboard.

My mother taught me about weeds and the names of the pretty flowers. She bought me lots of records with songs and stories, and I would listen to them for hours. I had lots of storybooks and could name the titles when my mother asked me. My mom and sister read lots to me. I think that's why I enjoy reading so much now.

I was a little scamp! Once I crawled into my brother Scotty's old Chevy and saw a little hornet's nest. I didn't know what it was so I hit it with a stick to find out, and the hornets came flying out and stung me. It hurt so much. I ran crying into the house. Mother covered my face with wet mud and soon it didn't hurt anymore.

I attended kindergarten at age six along with normal children and had fun with the things that were taught. The next year, instead of going on to first grade, my teacher, Mrs. Pugmire, said I should take kindergarten over again. I didn't stay long for the neighborhood kids made fun of me. At school they suggested that I go to a special training school to live. My family couldn't stand the thought of it, but Mama finally decided to try it for a year. My sisters came and got me every weekend because my mom didn't own a car. When they took me back, they always took lots of treats for the whole dorm.

After the year was over, Mama brought me home. She found out about a special class in the school district, and I began going to school again. I loved every minute of it. I was chosen to be "Jack" in the play, "Jack and the Beanstalk." Mrs. Brown taught me the ABCs and how to sound out letters and spell words. Mrs. Kimball taught me to read. I learned easy math: addition, times-tables, take-away, and division. My friends at school did such beautiful writing. I wanted to learn how, so Mama brought me some pretty orange paper, and I worked and worked every day learning to write cursive. I also taught myself how to type. (I know Heavenly Father taught me how.) I learned to crochet and make string and shag rugs, and the teacher sold some of mine. I went to school until I was eighteen, then I could no longer go because of my age. It broke my heart for I loved to learn things. I asked Mama, "Do you think they have school in heaven?"

My mom passed away with a heart attack in 1967 when I was twenty-three years old. That was the hardest night I ever had. I cried and cried. My sister, LaDawn, and her husband, Mel Farr, asked me to come and live with them. This is where I started to learn about genealogy. For some reason I had always wanted to know more about my grandfather, Michael James Fitzgerald. He died a long time before I was born.

Four years went by and when my sister was in the hospital giving birth to her fifth child, a little girl, I started writing letters to people I found on some of the family genealogy sheets. I asked for information about my grandfather. Some of them said the Fitzgeralds came from Ireland and settled in Missouri, but no one knew for sure. The family heard that Grandfather's mother's name was Mary and his two sisters, Mollie and Sadie, were schoolteachers, but we're not sure. My sister and I have looked and looked, trying to find out all we could.

My Grandfather Fitzgerald worked for a while as a ranch hand at the Ferguson Ranch in Ibapah in Deep Creek, near the Nevada border. (No records there.) After Mr. Ferguson died, his wife ran the ranch. She was the Sheep Queen of the state and was very rich. Her daughter, Mary Matilda Ferguson, was sixteen and very pretty. Michael James Fitzgerald, who was ten years older, asked her to marry him. They ran away together and got married secretly. Michael and Mary set up housekeeping at Felt ranch. (No records there either!) My sister and I found an old picture of some men on horses and others standing on the roof, but we don't know which one was my grandfather. The writing on the picture says, "Saloon on the Felt Ranch." We heard that Grandfather later became the saloonkeeper. Then we couldn't find anything more about him for a long time.

I looked for information on my other families and was able to find many records and gather the sheets together and start a genealogy book. I have been able to meet and talk to many relatives, some I had not met before. I love to meet new people!

One day I received a letter from California, from a friend, Charlene Hobbs. I met her while she was visiting friends here. She knew I was looking for my grandfather and how much I wanted to find him and his family. She drove many miles to a federal record center and found my grandfather! Michael James Fitzgerald and his family were living in the 1900 Census. This was our *first* record of him with his wife and children! I felt so happy! I was sad, too, for they divorced a few years later.

Sis and I talked to my great-aunt Daisy's daughter, Ruth. She told us she met Grandfather once when she was a little girl. He was living in a tent behind his daughter's home. He was very ill. She and her mother took him a bowl of soup. She remembered that he kept a little light burning as he seemed afraid of the dark. He died a short time later, before 1910.

Not long ago, my sis and I found an old news article that mentioned "Frank Fitzgerald, a member of the fire brigade." It said something about my grandfather: "Mike Fitzgerald, saloon keeper (the defendant's brother)" who posted bond for his brother Frank. I hope to find out more about my grandfather's brother, Frank Fitzgerald. Sometimes it seems like I haven't found very much on my grandfather's family, but I'm not giving up! I care about him so much!

Our family held a reunion where my brother, sister-in-law and family live. We all planned it together. I decided to make a small genealogy book for each brother and sister and all my nieces and nephews. I gathered what information I could on each family, made out sheets and found pictures of Mom and Dad and my brothers and sisters and their families to go in the books. It was a surprise for everyone. This made me so happy. I knew I was doing my Heavenly Father's work as I helped them to know about their families.

I have worked at two different stores for the handicapped. Now I work as a custodian at our church. I enjoy the young adult program at church. One summer we took a raft down the river which was really fun. We slept out in sleeping bags under the stars. Another time I was in charge of a Christmas program at a rest-home near the hospital. A friend helped me. We sang Christmas carols, read Christmas poetry and had a really good time. Two or three times a year my sis helps me have a party so my handicapped friends can come. We always have fun. My sis helps me with many things.

I hope I'll always be found doing the Lord's work. I find such happiness in antyhing I can do to further His work here on this earth.

I formed a group called "The Crusaders," inviting anyone to join the fight against pornography, bad movies and television shows. I print up petitions and hand out information and addresses so people can write and let the producers know how they feel about the programs.

I'm also gathering information on handicapped friends and plan to write a little book about them. I hope I can accomplish this as I love writing. I keep a journal and try to write each day. I'm on my third notebook. I keep my mind and hands busy trying to make the world a better place in which to live. I feel very blessed to be able to do the many things I do. I thank my Heavenly Father for giving me so many opportunities to work and have good friends and help others. In everything I do, I try very hard to be a faithful son.

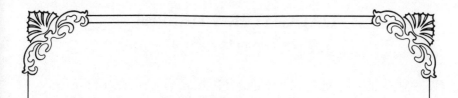

II

The Family Circle

DAUGHTER'S HELPER

By Tamara H. Fackrell

My mother, Margaret Walker Hudson, taught school for forty-four years. She cared for my dad, James Hudson, and me as well as kept up our home. I am very proud of her for these accomplishments. She always said the genealogy for her side of the family would be left for me because she didn't have time to do it, teaching all winter and attending the university almost every summer.

She did, however, pass on story after story of our ancestors handed down from grandparents, great-aunts and uncles, and cousins, especially stories of famous people. For example, perhaps being related to the founder of a famous university or to a signer of the Declaration of Independence really held my interest, in trying to prove these stories to be true. When the chance came to take a genealogy class, these stories spurred me on to learn the techniques of researching. I fell totally in love with genealogical work.

I soon realized I couldn't do it alone. It was overwhelming! My mom, now well into retirement, would *have* to help. But her usual response to my plea was, "You're doing fine. Just keep it up."

Finally one Saturday I scheduled a special trip to the genealogy library, and Mom agreed to go. I was surprised! I showed her a little about the IGI microfiche and how to look up census records. Then we settled down to three large microfilm reels of cemetery headstone inscriptions.

About ten minutes into her film, Mother exclaimed, "Here are some Walkers!" I didn't think too much about it until she began to read the names. The record gave the birth date, death dates and relationships of my third great-grandfather, Charles Walker, his wife, his parents (which we had not known before), two more children whose names we didn't have, and a granddaughter who had died in infancy. I was practically hysterical! What a find! After I explained to Mom the depth of her discovery, she was as excited as I.

Recently, for my mother's birthday, my dad and mom, my husband, Karl, and I went out to dinner together. Afterwards I mentioned to Mom I would be going to the library on the following

Friday. Her eyes literally lit up! "Do you think we could go back to those cemetery films?" she asked. Then she turned to Karl and said, "This gal is really getting me hooked on this genealogy stuff!"

I now have a valuable, well-trained convert to the cause, someone to help and encourage me in the genealogy work that is ahead. I am so happy that Mother has caught the spirit of this exciting work and can be with me side-by-side in this common interest.

"We're doing fine, and we'll keep it up!"

BRIDGE OF LOVE

By Kenneth O. Darby

We feel like a bridge. On one side we have ten children, and on the other side an untold number of ancestors, and they just won't leave us alone. My wife and I find that as we become acquainted with the lives, problems and accomplishments of our ancestors, we experience happiness in our own lives.

When we first married, Faye and I decided we wanted several children and would take as many as the Lord sent us. For more than fifteen years we have been trying to reach and teach, coordinate and orchestrate the increasing number of children in our family. As they started school and formed other associations, it soon became evident that home was only a place to get ready to go someplace else. When we realized this, we felt we had to do something to reverse the trend, so we prayerfully set about to make our school-centered family a family-centered family once again.

Probably our biggest challenge as parents is the need for enough time to spend with each child. These days there is a lot of talk about quality as well as quantity time. We try to plan quality activities which don't require a lot of time yet are meaningful to the family. This allows us to "meet the requirement" of spending time with each one. But time is a quantity, and quantity is also important.

Faye and I have developed a variety of ways to be closer to our children: by taking them to lunch or shopping, to run errands or visit a friend. I may take a child with me to the office occasionally to help with a small project. In our home the children help with many projects whenever the need or idea arises in our daily schedule.

The children nine years old or above are taught to cook and bake, wash and iron their own clothes, and clean their own rooms. We try to keep a positive attitude about their work. In this way they learn to get along with one another and help others. Once a week each of the older children is assigned a day to prepare meals, bake bread or carry out other family chores. Though Emily is just seven, she enjoys helping in the kitchen. Todd is nine but can already bake bread "from scratch."

For family recreation we enjoy camping, swimming, roller skating or bike riding together. On a fifth or sixth birthday each child receives a bicycle. Steve, who is ten, taught six-year-old Kevin how to ride.

Faye has lots of helping-hands, even Sarah, age four, who helps with little Jared. When one of these little ones is in distress, the child who is closest helps out. Jill, who is twelve, especially loves to babysit. During times of illness everyone pitches in.

This plan may sound ideal, but there are always challenges. We continually have to battle with our mistakes, squabbles and dissatisfactions and inattention. We explain to our children that we want to be united in purpose as we do things together as a family. The reward is that we all work together in an atmosphere that is more pleasant and congenial. The children feel this spirit of unity. We are becoming a family-centered family once again.

Through the years we have tried a number of times and ways to sustain the effort to find our ancestral family. I first began researching my father's Darby line, but I didn't know exactly how or where to start, Grandad and his father emigrated at different times from "somewhere" in England, and we have thus far been unable to trace their English origins. Each attempt has brought only a sense of frustration and failure perhaps because of ignorance, lack of time, road blocks, or deadends. Those years taught us that genealogical research requires quantity as well as quality time. Even though we were not always able to accomplish what we desired, we never lost the feeling that this work is very important.

A few months ago we changed our genealogical course. We started taking the children with us to the library to search for our ancestors. We decided to start with Dad's mother's Littlefair line which originated in Durham, England. Together we struggled to read the faded census films. To some it may not seem a way to share time with a child, to spend an evening with our heads in a microfilm reader, but our children, Kaye, Ann, and Ellen, have enjoyed it immensely. We were soon having to say, "Move over so I can see, too!" Faye and I have recognized that we are a bridge in some respects, uniting the generations. For those children we have introduced to this work now have the same burning desire as we to know about their ancestors. A week rarely passes without one saying, "When can we go to the genealogy library again?"

Perhaps, we haven't accumulated a great deal of information, but what we have found has been exciting because it is about our family, and we are all working together. It is also sacred because we have felt warmth, direction and approval from those ancestors that some feel are cold and silent.

Genealogy does take quantity time, and we must strive to accept that. We have found that spending even a small amount of time doing genealogy with the children is spending quality time. Probably the most reassuring thing to Faye and me is that now, from either side of our bridge of love, they just won't leave us alone.

THE DEPUTY TRAIL I

By Diane L. Deputy

My husband Wally's parents, Ross Joseph and Josephine Newman Deputy, were deaf mutes who communicated events in their own special way. Papa's eyes sparkled with admiration as he related in pantomine his boyhood memories of his father, Manlove Sylvester Deputy, a strong outdoorsman who lived in Arizona. Papa remembered when he was five years old, sitting on his father's knee, and being promised "when he grew up" that he would receive the huge diamond ring Manlove always wore. Then his parents divorced. His mother, Cora Belle, and the children moved to California. Saddened, Papa would tell of a message which came years later, while he was away. He had missed hearing from his father by minutes, and never heard from him again.

During family visits, Papa loved to bring out the old worn Bible and album of his mother's family. The Deputy and Jenkins names, written so long ago were embellished with notes, pictures and news clippings. Papa told us about his mother, Cora Belle and her little family, moving back to her parent's home in San Diego. Two of her baby boys were buried there. She later moved to San Francisco and waited tables to support her two sons, George and Ross.

Ross loved to tell of meeting Mama at a school for the deaf in San Francisco. After the great earthquake of 1906, Cora and the boys returned home to her parents. In later years Papa went into professional boxing and eventually returned to the Bay area. He joined a social organization for the deaf and met Mama once again! They loved to dance to the vibrations of the music. Ross and Mama were married, and told about the problems of raising three normal children, Wallace Ross, Blanche and Jackie, and how they took turns sleeping with a hand on the babies to "feel" them cry. As the children grew, they were taught to read lips and pantomime rather than "sign." They all matured, married and have families of their own. Sometimes Papa and Mama would say, "It is hard for the deaf." For Papa's sake it seemed I must try to locate his father or some record of his family.

I knelt and prayed for direction and that I might understand what do do. After re-reading all of the notations and clippings in the Bible and reviewing my notes, I still had only a name and two pictures of Manlove Sylvester Deputy; one young, slim, and proud with dark hair and even features, the other more mature with a handlebar mustache. Such a handsome man! His direct gaze showed great strength and resolute determination. What had happened to him? Why had he disappeared?

Papa was born in Phoenix, Arizona. Surely the family had been united then, but the Phoenix information operator informed me that *no* Deputys were listed there!

I remembered Papa mentioning his early years in San Diego. The San Diego operator gave me one name: Mrs. E. C. Deputy who responded by saying we were not related, but perhaps her deceased husband's brother might help. He lived in a small town near *Deputy,* Indiana! I wrote to the Postmaster of Deputy requesting that he direct my letter to anyone interested in the history of the family.

Meanwhile, I visited the genealogy section of the Los Angeles main library. A friend ran up to me with a small blue book which revealed several Deputy families of Deputy, Indiana! There was a paragraph about a Sylvester Deputy who emigrated from Wales to Delaware in the late 1600s. Was Manlove *Sylvester* Deputy named for him? I was overwhelmed! My first day at the library was a success! I felt very thankful. I wrote the author, Mary Osterman, who responded at once.

Several days later I received a letter postmarked Deputy, Indiana! Malcolm Deputy, a college student, writer and historian, promised to send me information he had compiled from cemeteries, church records, etc., and a few of his Deputy pioneer "parables" (as he called them). Finding no immediate tie, Malcolm recommended I write to Mr. O. D. Deputy of Brownsville, Texas, a relative of undetermined relationship, who had visited a Deputie shop near the Deputie River in Scotland!

The fine precise handwriting of Mr. O. D. Deputy was beautiful to see. His letter and pedigree chart revealed some interesting information that was surprisingly similar to the Indiana branch! He had once met a Mr. Jack Deputy who owned an electric shop in El Paso, Texas and suggested I write to him!

A couple of weeks after my El Paso letter was mailed, I returned home rather disappointed from a fruitless trip to the library. My neighbor, Mrs. Cooper, called out, "Mrs. Deputy, Mrs. Deputy, you had visitors today. They didn't say who they were," she said, "but their car had a Texas license plate!" It had to be Jack Deputy! Instantly I felt wonderful! That evening we visited with *our* cousins, Jack and Dorothy Deputy! Papa and Mama came too and were so happy! At last, we would learn the true history of our branch of the family tree!

Jack told of a visit his father, George, had made years ago to his brother, Manlove, in Arizona. The information gleaned from that visit was shared with us:

"Manlove and George Deputy left Michigan for Texas. George stayed in Waxahatchie, married Susie Kent and there I was born. Manlove moved west to Arizona and became a "mail-order" dentist on an Apache Indian reservation. He was a true outdoorsman, endowed with great physical strength. After his marriage and divorce from Cora Belle Jenkins, Manlove moved back to the reservation where he eventually remarried and continued his work. Manlove S. Deputy died in the early 1930s on the reservation somewhere near Three Rivers or White River in Arizona."

Jack Deputy then gave us a letter yellowed with age, written many years ago by Wally's grandfather. On the outside was a notation: "From Manlove Deputy, beter keep this as it was his last to me.-1905 Sarah M. Deputy, Niles, Michigan." The letter read:

Fort Apache, Arizona   November 21, 1905

Dear Mother,

I will write you a few lines, I have located at Fort Apache. I traveled overland from Grant, hunted and fished some. We have plenty of deer and turkey near here. Some of the boys brought in a bear and a load of Game. It is raining today so the mountains look gloomy and snow-capped in the distance. I believe I will be quite busy here as a great many have spoken ahead so as to have their teeth repaired before I leave. Two small rivers flow near this place and one through the Garrison. It cost me $15.00 a day for *teem* and men to bring me here. We traveled over some pretty country mostly mountains. Hoping you are well I will close as ever.

Regards to all, your son, M. Deputy

The next day Jack and Dorothy returned to Texas. Our precious visit with our new-found cousins was over.

I sorted out my jumbled notes. Excitedly I wrote the Arizona State Vital Statistics Office for the death certificate of Manlove, but no record of his death could be found. Meanwhile letters with other Deputy information were coming in from Malcolm and other correspondents. Ruth Enos Tennyson of Philadelphia, Pennsylvania contributed invaluable data and documents from Delaware. I added them to my ever-growing file along with other correspondence.

An impression to call the Bureau of Indian Affairs in Los Angeles netted me the address of the Phoenix branch. I wrote immediately! Their representative apologized for the lack of information about Dr. Deputy. The letter was signed, then a P.S. added, "One of our older employees just entered the office who remembers Mr. Deputy! He says that his *wife* is *still* living on the Apache reservation at White River, although Mr. Deputy passed away some years ago." I was so excited!

Mrs. Micah Deputy, a schoolteacher on the reservation at White River, Arizona replied immediately, "How strange you should write after all these years. Mr. Deputy died just twenty-five years ago today." She enclosed a small snapshot of Manlove. His genealogy was penciled on a folded piece of lined paper and written in his own hand.

Joseph Walton Deputy — "Father" (So, Papa, Ross
    Joseph was named for his grandfather.)
Born Sept. 30, 1828 at Milford, Delaware
Passed away April 28, 1881, Cass Co., Michigan

Sarah Matilda "Lane" Deputy — Mother
Born January 14, 1841 in Cass Co., Michigan
Passed away in Niles, Michigan in 1926

Manlove S. Deputy born June 13, 1862 in Cass Co.,
    Michigan
(written in another hand) — died July 13, 1934 at White
    River, Arizona

DIANE L. DEPUTY

George W. Deputy born in Cass Co., Michigan March
  11, 1864
Passed away September 18, 1919 at El Paso, Texas

Papa and Mama and the family were delighted with their new relatives, Jack and Dorothy Deputy, and the information gained from Manlove's widow. Jack promised to send us a box of old family pictures, etc., which he had stored in his garage. We looked forward so much to seeing them. Then we received a letter that a hurricane tore the roof off the garage and all the precious photographs had blown down the canal. It was a sad day. I had longed so much to see pictures of Joseph and Sarah Deputy.

One night I was given a special dream which consoled me. In the evening I was knocking at the door of a home much like our own. I seemed to know the pleasant older woman who invited me in. We walked down the hallway to the living room, and she led me over to a large drawing board. She watched intently as I studied a sensitive sketch of a handsome older gentleman. He looked so familiar! Suddenly, he was no longer a portrait, but a person standing by my side! He was so handsome and dignified, dressed in his dark suit with his long white beard and bright, piercing eyes that twinkled as he smiled. I felt love for the gentleman and his wife and their love for me. I was happy to be with them even for a short time. I awoke with a peaceful feeling. Somehow I had been privileged to be with Joseph and Sarah Deputy and did not grieve for the lost pictures anymore. My prayers had been answered an hundred fold!

Our Deputy genealogy had not only led us to Papa's father, but on a long, winding trail through Arizona, Texas, Indiana, Michigan, and Pennsylvania, then back to Delaware!

PUTTING FIRST THINGS FIRST

By Jeanne Spaulding

Genealogy brought my grandmother and me together after we had not spoken to one other for more than five years. How silly the disagreement seems, now that we have become reacquainted and are good friends. Our birthdays are on the same day, but fifty years apart, and we have discovered that we have much in common.

After my first few visits with Grandma, I learned that my Aunt Thelma had already been working on my Adkisson line and had traced it back several generations. She generously made copies of all her work and made it available to me.

I noticed that as I began asking members of my family about their ancestry, my husband, Al Spaulding, suddenly became very interested in his family lines. Soon we made a trip to Santa Barbara and obtained several generations back on the Spaulding line from a second cousin. It was great! Then Al's mother became interested and gave me several names and addresses of persons I could write about her mother's Best family line. Before I had time to write, however, I received several pages of Best history in the mail from other members of the family who had gotten the word via the grapevine.

When Al and I married, he was a widower with three sons. His first wife Virginia's family name was Dubose. I hadn't thought of looking for her genealogy, but one summer while we were traveling through the South, we visited some of her relatives. Many Dubose records came into my hands from the pages of their Bible and the family graveyard. I copied the information into a spiral notebook that I kept handy.

After returning home and becoming involved in other things, I never thought of those names again. All the other records we had collected, lay in a black binder on my desk, waiting for me to do something with them.

Around Mother's Day of the following year, I had a most unusual dream in which Al's deceased wife, Virginia, came to our home for a visit. She asked about her three boys, and requested that we not let them forget her. I realized that, in addition to being a good mother to these boys, one way to help them remember their mother would be to present them with her family records.

Immediately I began looking for her genealogy records that I had copied in Tennessee. I practically turned the house upside down but couldn't find them anywhere. I feared they were lost and earnestly prayed that they would turn up. Sure enough, as my daughter was cleaning out her room, she found the spiral notebook. Fortunately, she asked about throwing away the few written pages so that she could use the book. Thank goodness I went to see what she was talking about, and there was the Dubose genealogy. My prayers were answered!

About this same time I heard a gentleman named Fred Dellenbach give a very inspirational talk about genealogy. This made me want to work on my records again. It seemed I had been deluged with information from all sides but still could not find the time to organize my records. Now I had a plan to solve the problem!

I went home and asked my husband if I could spend a week with a friend who lived in another state near a genealogical library. On several occasions she had offered to help me with my research. I thought this would be an easy way to accomplish my goal. With my husband's permission, I planned a genealogical trip. He said I could drive if someone went with me. I asked Karen Dellenbach, daughter of the gentleman who was such an inspiration to me, and she said, "Yes." Karen wanted to work on genealogy, too, so we planned a pleasant week together.

On April 1st at 5:00 a.m. we left home. Before long it started to drizzle. We had a harrowing trip through rain, snow and blizzard, and at one point our car lost power and quit. I "hailed down" a sweet girl named Debbie who drove us into town. We had to have the car towed in and repaired. After losing a couple of daylight hours, we started out again. Not far on down the road we hit slick ice. The car started to fish-tail, we lost control and spun completely around, narrowly missing a pickup truck with a camper on it. It was a miracle someone wasn't hurt or killed. We stayed overnight at the next town then continued on our way. We were very aware of the principle of opposition as well as very thankful to the Lord for his protection through these trials.

I spent all day and part of the night just sorting through my records and trying to put them in order. At the library I began frantically checking for my family names but found nothing. Now I began to see why my work was so important. I also searched for additional census information but found very little. At times discouragement was so great that I had to pray for help.

While visiting with my researcher friend about my problem, she felt impressed to suggest that I stop searching for new names and start putting in order the names I already had accumulated. She helped me organize my work and pinpoint the information that was missing so that I could continue my search after I returned home. With the information I found in my own letters and records, I was able to identify some sixty names and add several new branches to my family tree! I felt a big load off my shoulders. We had sunshine all the way home!

The important lesson I learned from this trip is that the value of the records at hand must be realized and acted upon before searching for new names. Many people are praying for the Lord to open up their difficult research lines when they haven't done all they should with the records they already have. Within the last few years, with seemingly very little effort on my part, the amount of genealogical information that has come to me from unexpected sources has been absolutely amazing! The spiritual growth and development that has also come has blessed my life and that of my family.

It has been fun writing this experience and realizing all the blessings that have come from the things I have done: like making up with my grandmother; striving to be a better mother to both families of children; finding so many kind people that helped in time of need; and realizing that genealogy really is important.

MINA RUTH MUSE

MOTHER'S PRECIOUS TIN BOX

By Mina Ruth Muse

My grandfather, William Fleet Peterson, died of a bite he suffered while protecting a child from a rabid dog. His daughter, my mother, was heartbroken. She wrote several of his and Grandma's people in North Carolina telling them of the tragic circumstances of his death. That was 1929.

Grandfather and Grandmother, Margaret Bane Corbett, had been separated from the rest of their family for nearly 40 years. They left North Carolina in the 1890s and moved to Georgia to work in the turpentine mills. Both of Grandfather's brothers also moved to Georgia, although one later returned to North Carolina. Around 1900 my grandparents left Georgia for Louisiana, and never returned to the State of their youth. Thus, we never knew our Carolina relatives.

Answers to Mother's letters were carefully kept in a little tin cigar box, in her trunk, which we children were never allowed to open. As we watched her go through the trunk for other things we were especially curious about the little green box. She always gave an answer that satisfied us, so we never handled its precious contents.

Mother passed away in 1969. I thought then about gathering information on her family, but it was not until after my father's death in July of 1971 that I actually did anything about it.

When I began writing letters to the families of Mother's brothers and sisters, much to my surprise they all responded eagerly. Mothers kin seemed thrilled to be able to contribute to the family history and in return they hoped to receive information about Grandpa and Grandma's people. One reply mentioned that Grandfather had a brother who came to Louisiana and lived in Mansfield. Why, Mansfield was only forty miles from where I was born and raised! I remembered as a child going with my mother to a white frame house with a wide front porch. I felt that since Mother was so glad to see the woman who lived there, she must have been related to us. I got out the little green cigar box from Mother's old trunk and carefully read each letter. One dated 1952 contained not only the names, but the dates and places of birth of Grandfather's brother James Peterson, his wife Effie, and nine of their children!

I wrote to the postmaster in Mansfield listing all the names and asked if it were possible, would he please forward my letter to any of these persons. About two weeks later I received correspondence from a lady at the DeSoto Parish Historical Society. My letter had been turned over to her. She had known the family well, but they had moved to El Paso, Texas. I called the El Paso information operator, and she found listings for five of James' sons in the directory! As a result of this information, I soon learned that the entire family had moved there, but that Grandfather's brother, James Edward Peterson, had died when the children were young.

I was happy to learn that one of the children of James was compiling a family tree and wrote to her. When I enthusiastically asked if this daughter would make a copy for me if I sent some money, she wrote, "We don't want your money, just send your address." I did, and they filled a whole notebook with information and sent it to me. From this I started about forty to forty-five family data sheets, then sent them back to her for more information. For months she carefully wrote letters to all of these families, gathering what she could. When she gave me the address in North Carolina of a daughter of my grandfather's brothers, I wrote to her and received much helpful information. I then called Wilmington, North Carolina to see if Mamie Porter still lived there (letter in the box dated 1952). To my surprise, her telephone number was still listed. It was not until I talked to her that I really understood exactly who she was.

I next chose a letter in the box which had been written to my mother by a girl who at that time was visiting her grandmother. I later found out that her grandmother was my grandfather's sister. Since it was now 1975 and this letter had been written in 1929, I held little hope of finding her but decided to try anyway. I wrote her a letter explaining that I had found a letter from her written to my mother in 1929. On the outside of the envelope, I made a notation to the postmaster requesting that if he knew her married name or whereabouts, would he please forward my letter to her. Then I waited . . . by some miracle, she received it! She couldn't believe that she had written my mother way back in 1929! So, I sent her a copy, and she wrote back saying that she would do everything she could to help me.

By this time I had collected three addresses on my grandfather's side of the family and one on my grandmother's. Her niece, Thelma, and husband had also come to Louisiana when I was quite young, and through the years Mother and Thelma had kept in touch.

I began to encourage my brother to go to North Carolina to try to locate our people. He could easily afford the trip. I could not. Finally I came out and told him that if he would loan me the money I would go. There was silence on the other end of the phone for just a moment. Then calling me by his pet name, he said, "Minnie, you need a vacation. I'll tell you what. You make arrangements to go, and I'll *give you* the money." I told him that I would pay it back; but his decision was made. I then began to get nervous. I would be spending around a thousand dollars, and I had very little to go on but three addresses. I told him that perhaps I shouldn't go—what if I came back with nothing? His mind was made up, however, and nothing I could say or do would change it.

In October 1975, with a knot in my stomach, I took a plane to North Carolina. I forgot one of the addresses; so when I got there I went first to Thelma's house. I had only two other addresses to pursue. Then when I phoned Aunt Mamie Porter, a business answered. They told me they had had that number for quite some time. My heart sank. Thelma later got the phone number of the manager of the court where my aunt had resided, and he told me that Mrs. Porter had a stroke and that she was in a nursing home, but that her children still lived there in Wilmington. At random I called a Peterson in the telephone book who just happened to be her daughter-in-law. She in turn gave me the number of a daughter who promised to have all of the family at the nursing home the following Sunday. That left me with only the address of the girl who had written my mother in 1929.

As soon as I could rent a car, I left for her home in Burgaw, thirty miles from Wilmington armed with only a chart of my great-grandfather's showing the names of his twelve children and some of their spouses. In the meantime she had gathered up quite a bit of genealogy on Grandfather's sister, Molsey Jane Peterson Fisher. In the course of the conversation in Burgaw, I was told that another of Grandfather's sisters had lived at a resort town called White Lakes, but no one had seen any of her family for years. It was then five in the afternoon, and White Lakes was only nineteen miles away. I decided to leave immediately. They warned me that it would be night by the time I got there, but I couldn't believe it. I forgot that when the sun goes down in the south, it is dark because there is no light still showing from behind the mountains like at home.

I drove to White Lakes, but before I arrived it was pitch black. I stopped at a small store where I asked the clerk if she knew of any old cemeteries, and I told her some of the names I was looking for. She gave me directions for one cemetery but when I arrived there, I found that even with street lights on, it was just too dark. I called Wilmington from a telephone booth to let Thelma know I would not be back that night, then I walked into a restaurant. The only person in there was the Chief of Police. He was a friendly soul, and when he heard what I was trying to do, he offered to take me to some of the cemeteries as he had a flashlight. We visited two, but he said that he wouldn't take me to the third, for if we came in there at night, the man there would shoot me for sure. He said that if I would come back the next day, he would have one of his men take me to every cemetery in town, but I told him that wouldn't be necessary.

The next day when I went to the same store to buy a toothbrush, I mentioned to the clerk that I was still trying to find where the Russes were buried. She turned to a lady standing there and courteously explained to her what we were talking about. Mrs. Whitted turned to me and said, "Why I knew Miss Matilda (Grandpa's sister's name was Mary Matilda Peterson Russ), and I knew Mr. Winning, and I knew all their children." She went on, "In fact, my husband and brother laid him out the night he died. If I wasn't working, I'd take you to their old homeplace." She then directed me to a Mrs. Smith at the Whispering Pines Antique Shop who also knew the family and could tell me more. At the shop Mrs. Smith and her son gave me three more of the children's names. They then gave me the directions to the cemetery where Aunt Matilda, Uncle Winning, and their five-year-old daughter Katie were buried.

After I copied the information from the tombstones, I returned to the antique shop. Mrs. Smith said that although the family had left White Lakes, they still had a son living in Fayetteville, but if he was dead, his son, who sold real estate up there, could perhaps help me. How fortunate I was able to make those connections which I did. One year later Mrs. Smith and her son were both dead.

I drove the sixty-odd miles up to Fayetteville, arriving there at night. The first number I dialed was Aunt Matilda's eighty-three year old son. He invited me out, and then his son-in-law dropped by and told me to leave my address and he would send me what I needed. Later he wrote that he appreciated my getting him started again on the Peterson family history.

By this time information was coming at me so hard and fast that names and places were just becoming a jumble. Most of Grandfather's people seemed to have settled within a sixty-mile radius. I never met a stranger. I was welcomed into their homes, and it seemed that we had known each other all of our lives. I heard their stories and wrote history and genealogy so fast that I could not seem to keep the families separated.

The wife of my grandfather's nephew was very helpful to me. Grandfather's brother, John Dixon Peterson, had lived in their home during the last ten years of his life. He and his daughter-in-law were very close, and the family names and stories which were so familiar to her were invaluable to me. John Dixon Peterson had a daughter named Elizabeth Pemberton Peterson who was to have been married at age sixteen, but just before her wedding day, she became ill, died and was buried in her wedding dress on the day she was to have been married. Elizabeth was named for her father's mother, Elizabeth Horn, and grandmother, Mary Nancy Pemberton. Later I found a will abstract which told of a Pemberton woman who left something to her daughter Nancy.

I decided to visit the state archives in Raleigh, North Carolina to see what I could find. In the meantime, a cousin mentioned that a lady from Elizabethtown who worked at the Bladen County Courthouse was making a record of all the graveyards in the county. As I drove toward Raleigh, I kept passing signs which pointed to Elizabethtown. I had the strongest feeling that I should go there, but thought that I was just excited about meeting her, and that it was something that could wait. However, the feeling persisted, and after I passed the third sign and had gone on for about one-half mile, I thought that perhaps the Lord was trying to tell me something. I turned around and cut back cross-country to Elizabethtown. I walked in just as the lady was coming to work at 8:00 a.m. I found out that she was working on census records for Bladen County. Within five minutes after I met her, she showed me where the census had been taken on both sides of the Cape Fear River. There I found the names of my great-great-grandfather and grandmother and five of their children, one of whom was my great-grandfather.

While in North Carolina I visited the graves of my great-grandfather and grandmother and was also able to learn the stories of all the families of their children. I almost know by heart which of my grandfather's brothers and sisters each of these families belong. These people seem as alive to me as if I had known them personally.

From this research has come records of about two hundred-fifty families. The living descendants of these families have been promised copies of my great-grandfather and grandmother's records, and their mutual interest is drawing them closer together. It will cost a great deal of time and effort to run off copies and mail out these books; but from these experiences has come a tie never to be forgotten. I love these people, and now we truly belong to a family. It all came about because my dear mother carefully preserved the letters which were pertinent to her family's history, and even though they were kept in a tin cigar box, she passed on to me the feeling of their great importance.

TELEPHONE CONNECTIONS

By Lynett Sled Snyder

How *did* people manage before the invention of the telephone! Whenever I want to establish a family "connection," I pick up the telephone. My husband has a beeper so he can be reached on the job within moments. The phone is a way to keep close to our children at home, as well as the married children and grandchildren, and they with me. I keep in touch with my parents in this way, especially as serious health problems are a concern. I also use the telephone to make extended family "connections" in my genealogy work!

Sometimes while working on my family history, I will send a card or letter to a relative, but I really don't enjoy writing. I love to visit relatives, but it's such a long distance to Arkansas, Mississippi or Louisiana (to say nothing of Georgia, Tennessee, Virginia or the Carolinas). So, I do the next best thing and call them on the telephone!

The other day I received a letter from Mary Ellen Souter of Minden, Louisiana, whom I had previously called. She wrote: "I have done genealogy for almost nine years, and when I receive a letter it's wonderful; but there is something almost magical about a phone call. This is especially true since someone else saw my query and not you."(!) Yesterday, I was surprised to receive a call from Mary Ellen. Had I not called first, perhaps she would not have felt she could call me. Though we have only known each other a short while, we have already established a friendship!

A genealogical query in the Bradley County, Arkansas *Eagle Democrat* was placed by a woman named Pat Sled. My aunt saw the ad and sent it to my dad in California who sent it to me. I gave Pat Sled a call, and she said, in one of her letters, "I want you to know how much I appreciated your phone call last week. I was beginning to get down. I didn't think I was getting anyplace, and I was really discouraged. Now I am all excited and eager to get started again." Since receiving that letter, our two-year friendship and our genealogy has been strengthened by many calls and letters.

On a visit to Arkansas, my parents discovered a cousin, Ann Richard, who was working on our Fogle line. I telephoned this cousin who gave me the name of Wanda Colvin who had been researching the Hamiltons. Ann and Wanda have sent me much helpful information which added to both my mother's and father's lines. I always try to help others in the same way.

While working on my Brooks line I phoned a 90-year-old lady, Evelyn Brooks, of Fort Smith, Arkansas. Her husband's father, Thomas Brooks, turned out to be a brother of my great-grandfather, Barkley Brooks. Without her help I might never have properly identified him. She gave me a lot of information over the telephone that helped me find other relatives. A few days later I received a letter and some additional names and dates from this cousin. I was introduced to Evelyn by Maeola Hickman, a distant cousin (the Hickmans married into the Brooks).

Another call that brought me "oodles" of information came from a sweet fellow named T. L. Godfrey. When my cousin, Ann Richard, told me there were Godfreys living in Dumas, Arkansas, I picked up the phone again. I called the information operator and asked for any members of the family living in the area. There were only three, so I chose the one with the same initials as my family. When I phoned there was no answer, so I called T. L. Godfrey which turned out to be a great blessing. He wanted to know how I was related, so I told him about my great-uncle, Virgil Godfrey. He recommended I call his niece, Jaeleen, in Little Rock, an uncle "out west," and a Godfrey in Texas. T. L. was so friendly and helpful. I asked if he would mind sending copies of his family information, and offered to do the same for him. When I called back an hour and a half later with another thought, his wife said, "He's already gone down to make copies." A few days later I received in the mail a packet of eight to ten pages just choc-full of information on the Godfreys. His note read, "I was glad to hear from you. If you look hard enough, you can (always) find someone who knows someone you know." I am making a more complete book of records on the Godfreys to send to T. L. and I have it almost ready.

Randy Midgley from Overland Park, Kansas sent a letter to my dad asking for information on the Sleds. While I was vacationing in California, Dad gave the letter to me. I called Randy on the phone. Her grandmother, Effie Sled Clanton, is a granddaughter to my second great-grandfather, Etheldred D. Sled, who was born in North Carolina and lived in Tennessee, Louisiana and Arkansas! We discovered we had much in common and were of the same faith. I decided to surprise her and made up a notebook on the Sleds and

Clantons. Randy called me after her Grandmother Effie, had passed away. At the family get-together after the funeral, Randy showed the relatives the family book I had given her. It was passed around for a couple of hours. Everyone was so excited, and they all wanted to send information to be included in the book, too!

These examples and others have taught me that calling on the telephone shows people that I really care. The personal touch is worth a lot. It helps create a friendly, cooperative relationship. I feel that telephone talks can help establish strong friendships. Some new-found "cousins" have said, "If you ever get back here, we'll really feel hurt if you don't come by to see us." Cousin Randy and her family came to visit last year and recently she suggested we take a trip together through Arkansas and Mississippi to visit relatives and gather family history.

Some may feel that telephoning is too expensive, but I wait until the proper time on Saturday, Sunday or an early weekday morning when the cost is less prohibitive. In our family we really have to "pinch pennies," but I budget my money carefully. Because of this my husband, Steve, is very supportive in the cost of the calls and my genealogy work.

When I started doing genealogy a few years ago, I had only a few notes, pictures and records which I organized into a family notebook. Now, I have twenty-seven large binders filled with information on my direct and allied lines. I love the work, and I'm always looking for another family "telephone connection."

DELAYED REUNION

By Eugene Tuckett

My grandmother, Sarah Ann Gee Tuckett, was a strong-minded woman! When she married my grandfather, he was firm in another faith, and her mother did not take kindly to the idea. In fact, she *strongly* objected to the marriage, but Sarah Ann had her own ideas, and they included John Tuckett! Her decision caused a long-lasting rift between these families.

A hundred years later we were on our way to Montana, hoping to heal that rift! As the miles sped by, we had plenty of time to remember the past. Sarah Ann's father, Noah Gee, and his family, and later the Tucketts, had crossed the plains in the early 1850s with other pioneers moving west. They settled in Spanish Fork, Utah, then in 1856 the Gees moved north, and after a few years they were never heard from again!

Through the years I had often wondered why the Gees left so suddenly. Where did they go? Were there other descendants? Had my grandfather been a man of faith? For sixteen years my wife, Madge, and I tried to find some trace of Noah Gee. We knew so little for Grandmother Sarah Ann had died when I was just a child. We searched for years through deeds, probates, and unindexed census records; and even passenger lists of New York and Philadelphia ports of entry, but to no avail.

Then, in a little tattered box of Grandmother's, we found, among some papers, a few old pictures that showed a small town near Bozeman, Montana. It brought to mind a vague tradition that some of the Gees may have lived there at one time. Some letters had been sent years ago but brought no response. Perhaps some descendants might still be there! We decided to find out. On the side, maybe there would be time for a little rock hunting for my lapidary hobby!

Prior to our departure we enlisted the help of relatives, a few of them had some old letters. Putting it all together we came up with the following:

> Gr-grandfather: Noah Gee
>> Birth: 25 Jan 1807   Place: England
>> Death: 27 Sep 1880   Place: New York
> Gr-grandmother: Ann Moore
>> Birth: abt. 1815   Place: Pennsylvania
>> Death: abt. 1892   Place: Unknown

The names of ten children were given with approximate years of birth, but no places. Only Grandmother's facts were correct. Now, we had to prove whether or not this new information was accurate. As we anticipated our first major trip and research endeavor, our enthusiasm gained momemtum! We wondered, if we found any Gee relatives, would they accept us? After all, this family had been separated for nearly a hundred years!

Our journey was so pleasant we almost floated into Yellowstone Park. The road wound through the beautiful mountainous country of Montana, down into the fertile Gallatin Valley, and eventually to Bozeman. We arrived about 6:30 p.m. and pulled into a service station. My wife jumped out of the car and headed for the phone booth while I pumped the gas. She began leafing through the directory looking for Gee names. To our delight she found six names, and began calling, but no one seemed to be home. Surely, it just couldn't be that *no one* would answer! We had come so far!

As I stood outside waiting for the attendant, I watched my wife's expression. She looked bewildered, then her face brightened. Apparently someone had answered! A few moments later in the car my wife said that a woman had answered, her voice was not quite audible from running to answer the phone. She had listened politely but said she knew nothing of the people about whom my wife inquired. "But wait a minute," she said, "you probably should see my sister-in-law, Maude Gee. She lives about eighteen miles out on Reece Creek." She gave general directions to help us find the way. As we headed toward the creek, our conversation went something like this:

"Shall I turn here?"

"This must be the road."

"I'll bet this is the corner," or;

"That looks like the old school house." And so on. . . .

In the gathering dusk we turned and drove down a tree-lined lane by a large two-story farmhouse. At last, we had arrived! Only then did we question the advisability of calling at such an hour for (in our preoccupation) we had not had an evening meal nor located a place to stay for the night. Having come this far we decided to continue. A woman a little older than ourselves was feeding her cats by the back door. Just as we headed in her direction, she turned and went into the house! Had she seen us or was she trying to avoid us? Gathering our courage, we walked up on the porch. Bravely, I knocked on the door and waited.

Soon the same lady opened the door and met us with some reserve (a natural reaction since we were strangers in the dark). I cautiously stated our errand, then almost before we knew what was happening, we were invited inside to talk to the woman's mother, Maude Gee, who was about eighty-three years old. She was cordial and immediately seemed to understand our feelings and our deep desires to find our ancestors. "Cousin Maude" possessed a remarkably keen mind and memory. She began telling us all about her family history and *our* great-grandfather, Noah Gee, as well as reciting the names and (many) dates of all his ten children! We were amazed!

Soon we were invited to supper with the family. As my wife pitched in and helped Maude's daughter, Bessie, with the preparations, the atmosphere became more friendly. The white linen dining cloth was brought out, and the table set with the nicest china and silver. We enjoyed delicious fresh trout, hashed brown potatoes, garden vegetables and hot biscuits. Finally, Bessie announced the "Gee dessert" as she brought out the ice cream carton and set it smack-dab in the middle of the formal white table cloth. Maude was shocked, but everyone laughed and we knew then that the barriers were gone.

After the supper dishes were cleared away, we sat down and visited together about our mutual family connections and also told of our own background. All the while we were talking, a warmth of love and oneness seemed to encircle us. This feeling was also noted by the others present, as well as Maude, who announced that she *knew* her deceased husband, Hugh (Noah's grandson), was there with us! She felt that he, too, was pleased at the unity of purpose we all shared in our delayed reunion. Before we paused long enough to be aware of the time, it was midnight!

Nothing would do but that we should stay overnight with them. Before we retired, my wife expressed one of the vital concerns of our visit, "Do you have *any* idea where our great-grandfather, Noah Gee, is buried? We have searched for him all over the East." "Why, of course," was the quick reply. "Right here in Gallatin Valley! We can go to his grave in the morning." We were shocked!

Bright and early at 5:00 a.m. we were awake and ready for our next adventure. Though our surroundings were unfamiliar, as we met again with the family, the warmth of our kinship remained the same. We attended their Sunday worship service which, though different from our own, was impressive, and we felt a sweet spirit of unity there.

Later, as we drove toward the East Gallatin Cemetery, our excitement mounted at the thought of actually seeing Noah Gee's burial spot. Was it really possible that our great-grandfather had lived and died right here in this valley instead of New York or Pennsylvania as some of the relatives had told us?

At the cemetery, among the other stones, a large gray monument engraved with elaborate and detailed carvings came into view. Our spirits soared when we finally read the long desired data inscribed on the stone:

Noah Gee
Born Jan. 15, 1807 in England
Died Sept. 27, 1879

As we stood together at the grave of my great-grandfather, I reflected on his life. What kind of man was he really? Cousin Maude answered my thoughts, "He was a tremendous person," she said. "Good to his family, although none believed as he did. At his wife's insistence, they had left Utah for good. He stayed true to the faith he had accepted early in his life. When he died, his wife directed that all of his cherished religious books be buried with him "because he loved them so much." Noah Gee was a sweet, kind man loved by everyone," Maude concluded.

At last, through the goodness of these newly acquainted cousins, we had found my long-lost great-grandfather! This sacred moment which had brought our families together created a loving relationship which welded many members of the Gee family together in a firm bond.

Because of this wonderful experience, Cousin Maude, her two daughters, Bessie and Nan, and her son, Hugo, graciously assisted us in finding pictures and other records from Bibles, cemetery records and courthouses to help us document and record some forty separate families. We have also been able to compile accurate histories of the Gee family. After properly identifying Noah with his parents, nine brothers and sisters, grandchildren and spouses, we have been able to trace his pedigree three generations into England. One ancestral line, of which we were previously unaware, now extends into Ireland.

In addition to the love that has developed with this family, we have made the acquaintance of a large number of descendants of my great-grandfather, all of whom were previously unknown to us. We desire to continue our association with all of these people, both in this life and throughout eternity!

We have visited Reece Creek four times since the original trip and have never, except for the earliest episode, been able to drive to that near-isolated ranch without having to ask directions several times along the way. Even then, we would end up having to retrace our path for several miles and start again in a slightly different direction. As we look back on that first visit, traveling over country roads through a strange land in the near dark to a residence we had never before seen, we have a firm conviction that we were led directly to the right place.

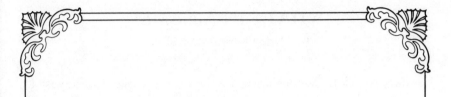

III

The Extended Family

MARIE OSTERGAARD GAISFORD

WHAT'S IN A NAME?

By Marie Ostergaard Gaisford

Los Angeles, California was my home. I was sixteen the year I first heard the name Gaisford. I was attending a youth meeting with some of my girlfriends. We had gone there to see if any interesting young men might be there that night, preferably college students, rather than the less interesting high school kids our own age. My girlfriend was hoping that she might see a certain young man who had played a violin solo a few nights before. Quite by chance she spotted the young musician accompanying a boy whom she had previously met. They both were well dressed and very nice-looking. We exchanged "Hello's" and "How are you's" and they introduced themselves. I caught the name of the one fellow, Jimmy Wells, but the young musician's name was strange to my ear, Walt Gisburg or something like that.

During the meeting our new acquaintances sat at an angle so I could see them out of the corner of my eye. I remember thinking that Walt Gisburg, or whatever his name was, was much too handsome to be interesting. I liked men who had something intelligent to say. . . but, of course, I hadn't heard him say very much so I really didn't know whether a violinist would be interesting or not.

After the meeting we joined friends around the refreshment table. We laughed, over punch and cookies, and talked of the fun times at school. The time flew by and soon the happy gathering dispersed. As I was going out the door, I felt a tap on my shoulder. I turned to find Walt "Gisburg" standing there. He asked me if I would like to go to a Valentine's Dance with him the next week. I mumbled a few words in response.

Walter courted me for five years in spite of our attending different colleges. During that time I met his lovely mother, his three brothers and a sister. His mother took over the responsibility of raising the five youngsters after the father's untimely death, when Walter was barely twelve years old! They were a wonderful family who had learned to make ends meet during a national economic crisis. Each child learned to work hard while young.

During our courtship years I became enthralled with Walter's stories about his mother's unusual family. Her grandparents were both prominent physicians, who had graduated from the Philadelphia School of Medicine in the mid-1800s. One of their daughters became a concert pianist and a son followed their profession of medicine. His wife studied culinary arts in France and opened her own School of Home Economics and later was on the faculty of the state university at the turn of the century.

Music was ingrained in this family's life. One notable attainment was his grandmother's singing career. She married a physician and their son became a thoracic surgeon. He combined his surgery with dexterity at the piano.

My husband obviously inherited some of their talents and traits. At age fifteen he performed in the Hollywood Bowl and would probably have continued in a musical career, had his uncle not advised him to develop his intellectual and humanitarian tendencies. Although Walter has enjoyed musical discipline all his life, his first love has been his profession of medicine.

Twenty-three years later we have fine sons and daughters, who carried with them the famous heritage of music and scholarship. They each have strong bodies, but such gentleness, that I wondered, "What could their Gaisford ancestors have been like to pass on such outstanding genes?" At that point I began my search. I wanted the Gaisford story to be part of our family collection.

I began first with my husband. He remembered that his father was a very kind person. He also knew that he was an electrician who worked for the motion picture studios in Hollywood, California. He had gone to many movie sets with his father and met many famous movie stars. He remembered that his father had several brothers who visited each other on a weekly basis. He couldn't remember much more than that. After his father's death his mother's family had no further association with the Gaisford line.

Next I went to my husband's mother for information regarding the Gaisford family. She was hesitant to talk about her late husband. She said the circumstances at the time were very difficult and she preferred not to talk about it. I was able, however to obtain the address of a cousin, and the address of the last living child in her husband's family. Even though none of these relatives knew me, they were all eager to get in touch with family members. I was able to get pictures of their families and newspaper articles of deaths, etc. Information on fathers and mothers, sisters and brothers were in articles and I was able to find other family members through these. In the newspaper clippings it gave information on professions and vocations. It was wonderful to be able to put pictures with histories. As I accumulated these things I found my children becoming very interested in all of their forefathers.

After months of work, I took all of these things to my mother-in-law. She was greatly pleased and she decided to tell me a little of her life with my husband's father. She wrote a short history about him and shared many pictures that had been tucked away for years. She had been hurt over bad feelings between some of her husband's brothers at the time of his death. She therefore estranged herself and her children from the family from that time on. By the time I started collecting things, the brothers had all passed away, and the bad feelings with them.

During the next year I learned that a diary had been found belonging to our great grandfather. It had been treasured by one of his daughters and secretly put in an old trunk. When she died, her daughter also hid the diary. In 1972 that daughter died. When her niece went through her things to settle her estate the diary was found. What a joy! It told who his father was, who his brothers and sisters were and where he had been born—Trowbridge, England. What fun it was to know my husband was English. His ancestors had been weavers. Personal histories I pieced together, revealed Gaisford family attributes of great generosity and selflessness. They were very special, honorable people.

In 1983 my husband and I were able to combine business with pleasure and go to Trowbridge, England to visit the town where his great grandfather had been born so many years before. We took lots of photographs of the beautiful country and the areas where they had lived. In the records of Emmanuel Baptist Church, we found marriage certificates, birth certificates, and death certificates which added to our history. The Historical Society of Trowbridge had recently published a book of old Trowbridge 1800-1950. We purchased one of these books and we are sharing it with our family here in the U.S.A.

During these past few years we have made contact with hundreds of families who are the descendants of our great grandfather, George Matthew Gaisford. Although we didn't know them by sight, we are combining their pictures and histories to go into one big book, *The Gaisford Family History*. It is really exciting to learn of past and present family members. It is like a big adventure into life. Each member has so much in common no matter when they lived on this earth. They all had stories to tell. All had different personalities and had lived in different places. I have seen and heard about these wonderful people who carry with them the name Gaisford. I can see why my sons are such fine young men. They have great forefathers. We have seen what is in the researching of a name; adventure!

MY TRAINING SESSION

By Robert S. Green

In January of last year I had the opportunity to train representatives of several European companies in the use of our computer systems. Before starting my trip I gathered some family information to take along in case I had a chance to do a little genealogical research (although I had no idea how to go about it). I recently learned that my great-grandmother, Catherine Curtis, who was born in Stoke Lane, near Leigh upon Mendip, Somerset, England, had been given to an uncle and aunt to raise when she was only one day old. Census searching in the usual places had proved fruitless. I knew only the names of Catherine's parents, Stephen and Sophia Bryant Curtis. I hoped to find more about this grandmother's family so I made it a matter of prayer. Perhaps I might even have time to visit some of the places my ancestors lived! These were my thoughts as I prepared to leave on my journey.

ROBERT S. GREEN

I flew first to Atlanta, Georgia, then boarded an international flight to Europe. Upon arrival at the Frankfurt airport I was met by our German representative. We had a pleasant journey driving south through many picturesque towns on the way to Geneva, Switzerland. There I was introduced to the manager of the group, Denis Bony. It turned out we were members of the same church, so we felt we had a lot in common. In the evenings after the training sessions were over, we toured the city, and he showed me many historical points of interest.

My next assignment was in Scotland the following Monday, so I had a couple of days to spare. I flew to London for the weekend, toured the museums of art and natural history and other famous sites, then attended Hyde Park chapel on Sunday.

I stepped off the plane Sunday evening in Glasgow, Scotland. It was necessary to take a taxi about thirty miles to my hotel, an antiquated interesting-look building. The next day I met our sales representative, John Kelly. We worked through the day, then decided to have dinner at the hotel. During our conversation John related a little history of the hotel and the area. I happened to mention that most of my ancestors came from England and told him of my desire to do a little genealogy in London (before leaving for Germany). To my amazement Mr. Kelly interjected, "Oh, is that so? My father and I are both avid genealogists!" I went on to relate how I hoped to find the parents of my great-grandmother (their marriage and children). John then proceeded to tell me the precise way to look for the information I needed! There was a building in London, he said, called St. Catherine's House, where all the marriage records were kept. He also told me of another where the birth records were housed. By the time dinner was over, I had been given an exact plan of action!

As it turned out, I finished my work in Scotland on Wednesday. I flew back to London, and by Thursday I was ready to work on my genealogy. My sightseeing tour was postponed. (My great-grandparents meant more to me than any worldly pleasures I might enjoy!) Due to the excellent map and instruction I received from my business associate, I *was* able to find the marriage records of my great-great-grandparents in only thirty minutes (not counting traveling time!)

Stephen and Sophia Bryant Curtis were married 2 January 1855 in Salperton, Glostershire, England. Stephen, the laborer, was listed as a widower, the son of Richard Curtis, the butcher. Sophia's father, Charles Briant, was a gardener. Just finding this one document added two generations to my family and a new place to continue my research. I felt greatly rewarded for my efforts. The following two days I went on to search the birth records (and am still working to complete details on that family). I left for Germany with a very satisfied feeling.

A short time later John Kelly visited me in America. I was able to take him on a tour of our genealogical facilities which was a nice experience. I recently heard that he left the company some two or three months after I was there. Looking back on my European experience, including all those training seminars, I feel sure the Lord answered my prayers and sent a genealogist to train *me* at the precise time I needed it!

THE DEPUTY TRAIL II

By Marilyn Deputy

In 1968 when I was a sophomore in high school, Grandma Josephine Deputy passed away. Grandpa Ross Deputy followed four years later. We sorrowed at the loss. Sunday dinners at Grandma and Grandpa Deputy's home had been a family ritual since my childhood.

As a youngster, I was never particularly interested in my heritage, although I picked up bits and pieces of genealogy from family conversations. As I matured, I began to assist my mom with research on some of her ancestral lines—Bolins, Bowies and McDaniels. In 1978 I began employment as a genealogical librarian. Often people would ask me about my surname. "Deputy," they would say, "that's an unusual name. Where does it come from?"

"My ancestors are from Michigan and Delaware. The original

immigrant was supposedly from Wales or France, but we've been unable to prove the lineage," was my standard reply.

After four years of giving that answer, I decided I'd better investigate the history of my surname. The next time I visited my parents, I queried my mom about the Deputy research. She shuffled through a couple of closets and emerged with a large bag full of documents arranged in folders. "Here's everything I have on the Deputys," she said and handed me the bag. "I did some research on Manlove's father, Joseph Walton Deputy, but I never could prove his father. There are so many Deputys in Delaware with the same names. It's confusing."

I decided to start my research with Grandpa Deputy's father, Manlove Deputy, the Indian reservation dentist. In spite of Mother's research, there was so much we did not know about his life. I tried to contact Manlove's second wife, Micah, but my letter was returned as "undeliverable." Over twenty years had lapsed since her correspondence with my mother. I presumed she might have passed away. I wrote for her death certificate which came by return mail.

The informant on the 1965 certificate, Mary Wicklund, listed her residence as Mount Pleasant, Michigan. I dialed the directory assistance operator. A Wicklund family was listed, so I made a call. A woman answered. I explained who I was and what I was seeking. "Aunt Micah's death? That was almost twenty years ago. Family heirlooms, photos, diary? Yes, Doc Deputy was a good husband to Micah. Yes, there were some books and personal belongings of Doc Deputy's life for Joseph to pick up. I'm very busy now and really don't have anymore time to talk. Just write me a letter, and I'll see what I can do." We ended the conversation. Micah and Manlove never had children. My grandpa's name was Ross, and his only surviving brother was named George. Who was Joseph? I was confused.

Mary proved to be as good as her word. An exchange of letters and photos brought the realization that Manlove Deputy had an *additional* wife and two sons, James and Joseph. Micah was actually his *third* wife!

Mary gave me a Los Angeles address where Joseph Deputy was living in 1965. I searched current Los Angeles phonebooks, and I *did* find a listing for a Joseph Deputy. A carefully-worded letter was mailed the next day. I received a warm reply from Joseph's daughter-in-law Norma. "Joseph Deputy passed away eight weeks ago, and your letter was forwarded to his only son, Dr. Robert Joseph Deputy. I am writing to tell you we were dumbfounded with your news. Manlove, indeed, was Joe's father, a dentist on an Indian reservation. We have Manlove's violin and his dental certificate from the University of Michigan. We had *no* idea he had been married before." Norma forwarded my letter to Joseph's only brother, James, who was still alive. He, too, was astonished to learn he had half-brothers. Perhaps the greatest irony of the whole situation was that Grandpa Ross, who had always longed to know his father, and Joseph, who kept in touch with Manlove throughout his life, lived within ten miles of each other for almost twenty years! If only they had known.

Uncle James and I corresponded. In the summer of 1983 James and his wife, Carnell, passed through our city on a vacation. My parents and I spent an enjoyable evening with them. I plugged in a portable tape recorder, and James reminisced about his early childhood on the Fort Apache Indian Reservation in White River, Arizona. James vividly remembered a small black metal box which his father kept under lock and key. He commented that the box might have contained family papers or personal belongings relating to his first family, but Manlove never allowed his wife or children to see its contents.

James' visit reminded me that I needed to find the records of Manlove's parents and grandparents in Delaware. I began by reading all the Delaware and Michigan documents my mother had collected. There were wills, land deeds, census extracts and tombstone transcriptions, but nothing mentioned Joseph Walton Deputy's father. The best clue I had was the 1860 U.S. Census of Michigan. Joseph Walton Deputy was living with Lovina Deputy (widow of Sylvester according to the land deeds). She was old enough to be his grandmother. Since I knew the family came from Delaware, I began searching Sussex County records for Sylvester. That created a problem!

The original Deputy immigrant to America, the forefather of all the Deputy families in the United States, was Sylvester Deputy, born in Wales about 1689. He fathered six sons and five daughters, several of whom named their sons Sylvester. Of course, these children also named one of their children Sylvester. Sussex County records were replete with Sylvester Deputys. How could I ever figure out which one was mine? I decided there was only one way. I would have to put together *all* the Deputy families in Delaware and identify my direct line by process of elimination. It would be time consuming, but since all the Deputys descended from the original Sylvester, I concluded I was at least gathering information on distant cousins and relatives.

I began systematically extracting the information on *every* Deputy in *every* available record of Sussex County. Meticulously, I copied the information onto family record sheets, many of which had been compiled and sent to my mom years earlier by Malcolm Deputy of Deputy, Indiana. If Malcolm had not compiled a family record sheet, I filled one out. If one existed, I simply added the information and source document, noting any discrepancies. I followed the same process with the letters and records of Ruth Enos Tennison of Philadelphia, Pennsylvania, a faithful correspondent of my mother's. Of special interest was a huge chart she had compiled listing many descendants of the immigrant, Sylvester Deputy. Several other letters added more.

At one point in the research process, a friend stopped me as I lugged my records to the Genealogical Library. "What are you doing with all that?" she queried.

"Well, my second great-grandfather was orphaned when he was a small boy. Since I couldn't figure out my direct line, I decided to put *all* the Deputy families together and see where he fits."

She shook her head, "That's not even reasonable."

"Maybe not, but I'm having a good time."

Two years, two notebooks and 300 family record sheets later, I have put together my direct line. Joseph Walton's Deputy's father was Joshua Deputy, husband of Mary Walton. They had at least five children but only Joseph and Zachariah lived. Mary was the daughter of Joseph Walton for whom Joseph Walton Deputy was named. My research thus far shows that Joshua was the son of Jesse, the son of Sylvester Deputy, the immigrant.

I am grateful this has been an arduous task because I have become acquainted not only with Manlove, Joseph Walton and Joshua Deputy, but with their entire extended family. The majority were seafaring men—oystermen and shipbuilders. The rest were farmers and husbandmen. Though only a few physical descriptions are recorded, I imagine that in their youth, most were strong and tanned from a life of physical labor in the sun. As they grayed with age, they probably never totally lost their bronze color.

Through reading 200 years of Sussex County records, I have become acquainted with the families of Walton, Manlove, and Beauchamp; Hudson, Truitt, Townsend and Clendaniel. Their lives intertwined with the Deputy's.

I now comprehend not just a few isolated families, but an entire society who lived during a 200-year period. I have gained a great respect for the gentle rhythm of life, the anticipation of youth, the trials of parenting and the mellow reflection of age. This understanding helps me to meet the demands of my own life with perspective and proper priorities.

More importantly, I have come to know and love all of these people. I have cried while reading court suits and divorces. I have admired the courage of some who pioneered frontier settlements. I have mourned at the death of a young parent. The compassion gained has aided me to reach out to others with greater tolerance and understanding. This depth of perspective and breadth of compassion helps me understand that we are all God's children.

PUTNAMS PROVED

By Glen R. Shaw

My great-grandfather, Thomas Howard Putnam, said that he was a descendant of General Israel Putnam of the Revolutionary War. My research, however, shows that our family does not descend through that line.

GLEN R. SHAW

During my first year as a teacher in Evanston, Wyoming, I became friends with a man named Read Putnam, an experienced genealogist. He began corresponding with my grandmother, Maude Putnam Shaw, who was famous for remembering every name, date and place of the family. We soon realized that, although Read and I had the Putnam name in common, it didn't necessarily make us related for we descended from different ancestors. We became good friends, however, and often played chess together.

After I moved from Evanston a year or so later, Read Putnam's wife was clerking in a local store. She was approached by an out-of-town traveler who noticed the Putnam name on the name tag she was wearing. He volunteered some information about a gentleman in Illinois who had collected material and published a book on the Putnam family.

Read was really enthused and followed up on the lead by writing to Illinois and receiving a copy of the book. Then he discovered it was not his family line. Since he had been in touch with my grandmother about the Putnams, he sent the book to her. Meanwhile, I learned of the incident and about the book, and I wrote for a copy!

The Putnams of Wabash County, Indiana by R. G. Putnam of Eldorado, Illinois was published in 1948. It contained *our* line in the book. From Daniel the line extended back through Howard, then Samuel Putnam and others of the Revolutionary War, but General Israel Putnam was not among them. The line continued back to William Puttenham, 1430-1492, of Puttenham, Tenne Sherfield and Warbleton, Buckinghamshire, England.

I have often felt since that it was more than a coincidence that I chose to live in Evanston that year, and that I was meant to find this book. I certainly feel that Read Putnam, the out-of-town traveler and my grandmother, who is now 103 years young, were all inspired to help me.

DILIGENT DAUGHTER

By Doris P. Westcott

When my cousin sent copies of her research on my father's line, it was the beginning of my genealogy hobby. I had always been interested in our family history. I had often questioned my grandparents who told me many true stories that sparked my interest. When I heard of my cousin's work on my father's line, I wrote to her. Later I offered to help and to exchange information. Since receiving the records, I have been inspired to go ahead on my own. I have written and received many letters, placed ads and queries, and joined historical and genealogical societies at home as well as in my research areas—and even hired a researcher for some specialized work. And I am having great success!

I also became interested in the work of the N.S.D.A.R. (National Society of the Daughters of the American Revolution), a patriotic genealogically-oriented organization. By documenting my own family connection to the already proven line of Revolutionary soldier, Michael Fry, I became a member. I checked my records and found it possible to document my connection to *several* such Revolutionary ancestors and to have the information published in the D.A.R. Patriot Index. To obtain additional information I consulted those volumes at the library and wrote for copies of the member's records which gave me the ancestor's lineage, documentation and descendants. I received several in the mail and found them very helpful.

In order to prove my Evans ancestor I wrote to the State Archives of North Carolina where he served. They found not only his pay-papers, but his military court record. I was amazed to find that such documents still exist! With these and other records I was able to open, prove and submit this brand new line to be included in the D.A.R. Patriot Index, and it was accepted! Line after was completed until I now have twelve bars on my D.A.R. ribbon, representing twelve documented lines back to the Revolutionary War!

What of my ancestors who had not served in the Revolution

because of age, infirmity, or religion? Did I feel less love and concern for them, less motivation to research and document their lives? What of the immigrants who came after the Revolution? I thought of one of my own ancestors.

In the 1780s a young lad in his teens left the comfort and safety of his parents' home in Belfast, Ireland to travel to an unfamiliar land, America. He became my fourth great-grandfather, John Laird. He was one of eight boys and two girls born to John Laird, Senior and his wife, Elizabeth Armstrong Laird.

It is surmised that young John came to live with Elizabeth's two brothers, John and Martin Armstrong, who had left Ireland for America and settled in North Carolina. John taught school for several years and eventually married Anna Marie Dorothea Frey Tuttle, a young widow with two daughters.

The Armstrong brothers fought in the American Revolution and received much land in Tennessee. So, in the early 1800s John and his family also made the trek to what is now middle Tennessee, purchased land and built a home in Giles County. In April of 1985 I had the privilege of visiting the old Laird house in Tennessee and walking on the floors that at least four generations of my ancestors had walked before me. The house was in the process of being restored by a young couple who had purchased it. As I stood in the actual home, I could not help but wonder about its former occupants and recall some of the history I had learned.

John Laird built a log cabin for his family to occupy while the larger brick house was being built. Slaves formed the bricks and did part of the building. The house was designed with four large rooms downstairs, a fireplace in each room and four smaller rooms upstairs. To the back of the house, and now connected to it, is the summer kitchen. Each downstairs room has a cellar. The walls are four bricks thick, and the floorboards are one and one-half inches thick and six to eight inches wide. From the cellar one can see the rough cut of the logs from which they were carved. In this house John and Mary Laird reared five girls and four boys.

In addition to farming the land, John Laird built a general merchandise store across the road from his home. He also became the local postmaster. In later life he retired to enjoy the comforts of his home. His hobby was birds, and he kept several cages of wild birds in his room. One of the slaves cared for the birds. Twice-a-day another slave took John to the sulphur wells to drink the water which he enjoyed.

John Laird's oldest daughter, Nancy, through whom I descend, was born 31 May 1793. She married James Hampton Evans, son of Edward and Martha Hampton Evans of North Carolina. Edward was courtmartialed during the Revolutionary War, but tried and cleared of all charges. Nancy and James Hampton Evans lived in Giles County, Tennessee at Evans Branch. Just down the road from John Laird's brick house is the family cemetery. It is located on a knoll covered with tall trees and surrounded by plowed fields. The weeds are almost knee high and some stones have fallen to the ground. One of these bears the inscription:

In memory of John Laird
Born March 17, 1770
Died December 27, 1861

Standing next to this stone is another which says:
Sacred to the Memory of Mary Laird
Wife of John Laird
Born September 20, 1768
Departed this life December 16, 1864

Other faded writing was not decipherable. Buried nearby are several of the children and grandchildren of John and Mary Laird. Among them are found the graves of two more generations of my ancestors!

My grandfather, John Laird, was a hardy pioneer, traveling over waters and braving the wilderness to help settle the land, but what was he really like? Was he religious, tall or short, kind or stern, generous? These questions may never be answered, but I will keep searching.

Perhaps I may consider myself a faithful daughter, diligent at compiling my father's and mother's histories as well as a dedicated member of the Daughters of the American Revolution. In the meantime, I have submitted papers on two additional Revolutionary ancestors to the N.S.D.A.R. in Washington, D.C. I am waiting to hear if my documented research on these lines has been accepted.

THE PEWTER PLATE
By Gladys Muller

My mother-in-law, Martha Theis Muller, was a remarkable and a much loved woman. She and my father-in-law, in their retirement years, lived in her family's old homestead, a rambling sixteen-room house in Germania, Pennsylvania. Germania was first settled by German immigrants in 1855 when William Radde formed a land company and lured buyers to the area by advertising in German newspapers throughout the United States. Two of Martha Muller's ancestors responded to Radde's appealing invitation to establish a German community in north central Pennsylvania. The old house was built by one of the ancestors. Because it was so large, there was never a need to throw anything away. It became a treasure trove of family memorabilia.

One of the things that made Martha Muller so remarkable, she had a detailed knowledge of several generations of her family, although she had never searched an archive nor sent away for documents. She had listened carefully to the family story-tellers and she remembered the wonderful old stories. She did things like labeling all the family treasures, identifying everyone in the old photos, and dating all the newspaper clippings. In addition, she gave each of her children an inventory of all the family items in the house, indicated their significance, and where they could be found. She hid many of the treasures away when the family was gone out of town.

After my mother-in-law's death the families of her two sons gathered in the old house to divide the family treasures. In one hiding place we found an unidentified pewter plate. It wasn't on any inventory, and none of us had ever seen it before. Closer scrutiny found that on the rim of the plate was inscribed the initials I.B.B., along with the date 1804. The only other marking was a logo centered on the back of the plate. We knew that the plate must be an heirloom but were mystified. Why had Martha not listed it? We thought, perhaps even she didn't know its significance; perhaps she only knew it was a family treasure.

Since I had been doing the research to back up my mother-in-law's oral history, the family suggested that I try to find out something about the plate. I returned with it to our home in Whittier, California and started by questioning anyone who knew about antiques, hoping to find a book of logos. I soon discovered that the antique dealers in America whom I contacted knew nothing about German pewter, and that the museums and art dealers knew even less! Finally, the County Museum of Art gave me the address of the German National Museum in Nurnberg. I sent a copy of the logo to the museum and asked for their help in identifying the plate. Very soon I had a reply. The plate had been made in the town of Fussen in the state of Bayern (Bavaria), in southern Germany. They suggested that I write to the Heimatmuseum in Fussen for more information.

Meantime, I scoured my records looking without success, for a person whose initials were I.B.B. Then I recalled that in earlier times the alte Schrift letters I and J were very similar. If I changed the I to J.B.B., they could be the initials of John Berhard Burnhauser who was my mother-in-law's great-great-grandfather. Surely this was the solution! Although we knew very little about this ancester other than his name and that he was born in Germany, he could have been alive in 1804. His grandson had emigrated to America and eventually settled in Germania, Pennsylvania.

I wrote to the Heimatmuseum of Fussen, and sent them the logo. I asked if Johan Bernhard Burnhauser lived in that community in 1804. I received a letter signed by the mayor, telling of their search through the city archives and church records on my behalf. They told me that the plate was made by Carl Ahorn, whose family had been pewter craftsmen in Fussen for three generations. More importantly, they sent me a three-generation chart of the ancestry of Johan Bernhard Burnhauser who had been born in the town in 1764.

In this rather unconventional way I found the answer to one of the most difficult questions in genealogy: the name of the parish in

Europe where a branch of my family once lived. I discovered that Fussen, in the state of Bavaria, lies close to the border of Austria. Its history can be traced to the Crusades when this town guarded the pass through the Alps. The famous castles of Neuschwanstein and Hohenschwangau are on the outskirts of town. How lovely to have one's ancestors come from a place steeped in beauty and history.

I often wondered why my mother-in-law, with her concern for detail, made no note of the plate. She knew about Johan Bernhard Burnhauser's existence; it was she who told me about him. Perhaps it was the "I" instead of the "J" that fooled her, or perhaps her grandfather never told anyone that he sentimentally brought that old plate to America when he emigrated. I wonder if my mother-in-law had known about the plate and had identified its original owner, would I have set out on my quest that resulted in locating the town in Germany where the Burnhausers lived for three generations.

The logo found on pewter plate:
F — Fussen, town where pewter mad
K — Karl
A — Ahorn (pewter craftsman)
Three running legs are on the
city crest of Fussen

A HELPING HAND

By Lorraine S. Hayes

Thanksgiving 1975 was a special one for me for I had been invited to spend the holiday at the home of my daughter, Marian Jensen, in Arizona. She met me at the plane in Phoenix, and as we traveled the fifty miles to her home in Arizona City, she told me about her neighbors, the Codys.

Marian told me that Bill Cody was a French Canadian who was so interested in finding out who his Cote ancestors were that he and his wife had made four trips to Quebec, Canada trying to find information from family members as well as the Catholic priest. The Codys had showed Marian the information they had collected but said they did not know what to do with it. They wanted to find someone to continue the research for them. Marian told them, "My mother has been doing genealogy work for twenty years, and she is coming for Thanksgiving. I'm sure she'd be happy to help you."

So, my first stop on arrival in Arizona City was the Cody home. How interesting it was to hear how his ancestor, Jean Cote (born about 1610 in France), came with others to Quebec, Canada in three small vessels. When a ferocious storm arose and they were all afraid they would drown, they asked God to spare their lives. They promised Him that in return, wherever they settled in Canada, they would build a church and that two members of each family would dedicate their lives to Him. They arrived in Quebec about 1634 where Jean Cote married Anne Martin. They settled in St. Anne Beaupre, Quebec and raised a family of five sons. They built a small church on the south side of the river, and it still stands today. The original benches have been worn smooth with use, and one has to be careful how he steps for the aisles are worn down lower than the hardwood knots in the floor.

As each of the Cote sons married, they spread out over the land, some having as many as twenty-five children in one family. At last count, there had been a total of two hundred priests and four hundred nuns in this family, so you can see they kept their promise.

When Bill asked me if I would do this genealogy for them, I

accepted without hesitation. Since I knew no French, I hired a qualified researcher, but when six months went by with no results, I decided I would give it a try myself! I always make genealogy a matter of prayer for I know I can't do anything without the Lord's help. I made my first trip to the Genealogical Library, knowing only a few names and places. I started with the card file to help me evaluate the Canadian records. Amazingly, name after name appeared in the parish register books. I found enough to keep me busy for about eight hours just copying the information. I took it home and worked for a whole week organizing the families and filling out pedigree charts. I felt my prayers were answered. Then I went back for more.

On my second trip to the Library, as I was getting settled at the table and preparing to find the books I wanted, a young man sitting next to me said, "I see you are working in Quebec. These books will be a great help to you. You may use them with me." I gratefully accepted his offer. I opened one of the volumes* and found a collection of thousands of French-Canadian names and dates that had been extracted from the parish registers and organized into families. Among the seven volumes I found many generations of direct-line families! Again I worked for hours copying the information, then took it home to sort it out.

On the third trip as I walked to the card file, I pulled out the Quebec drawer and placed it on the table. In a few moments a young lady came over to me and said, "I see you are working in Quebec. May I see your pedigree chart and perhaps I can help you." We found a place to work, and I showed her my records. Walking to the Canadian section she pulled several books on Canadian history from the shelves and placed them in front of me, smiled and walked away saying, "Have fun." They were very helpful. She came back several times to see how I was doing and gave me help when needed. The Cody family records were certainly multiplying at a rapid rate! I could hardly keep up with it all!

---

*Dictionnaire Genealogique des Familles Canadiennes by L'Abbe Cyprien Tanguay, A.D.S.

The next time I was in the library I recruited this same young lady who I had learned was working for her certification. The following day we worked together for ten hours. She checked over what I had done and was very surprised at how much I had found. She then showed me a new little book from Quebec that the library had just received and suggested I check it before I left.

About eight that evening we had accomplished much but were stymied on one line. The Codys had told me that this family had not come to Quebec with the first settlers. The young lady tried to find them in the French records, but having no luck she finally said, "I don't know where else to look." So, we decided to give up on that line. When I had finished everything else, I said to her, "Where is that little blue book you were showing me when I first came in?" She directed me to a certain shelf, but the book was nowhere to be found. While still searching for the missing book, I found a section of Canadian family histories. That was the first time I had heard of the family books, and as I looked at them, I became really fascinated, reading all the titles, but finding no little blue book.

While glancing down to the next shelf, I noticed a small book entitled DUGAY. I thought to myself, "That's French," so I took it from the shelf. I opened it up and was startled to find the very name we had just given up on! I could not believe my eyes when I saw the records of Francois Chasse, his wife, and family extending back three generations into France. Even now it is hard to believe this really happened to me! So the research continued like the blossoming of a fragile flower, one petal at a time.

Thanksgiving 1976 I again accepted my daughter's invitation to come for the holiday. This time a precious cargo of 210 Cote and allied surnames went with me. We had extended many lines on the pedigree back to the ninth, and some to the twelfth generations, into the 1500s—three hundred hours of accomplishment.

Since then Mrs. Cody has copied and compiled all the family group sheets into an extensive Book of Remembrance which is very precious to the family. How happy this must make M. Jean Cote and his wife Ann and their descendants to be so specially remembered.

As I look back and think of the fear I had of researching in another language, I am amazed at how easily it all came about with the Lord's help and persistent effort. I shall always remember that if we go as far as we can, God will give us a helping hand.

SUMMER OF SEVENTY-TWO
By Sandra Hull

The events of the summer of 1972 are exciting to recall! In April Grandmother's passing necessitated Mother's return to Long Island, New York. I decided to go along to help with Grandmother's affairs. Since Dad's family had lived for generations on the eastern tip of Long Island, we planned to include some genealogical research as well. One month to prepare was so little time, I realized. I first reviewed the family records to determine how to proceed. Mother and I contacted by letter all relatives who might have pertinent family information to let them know of our plans.

A short time later, Mom and I flew to New York and began to interview aunts, uncles and cousins who lived near Grandmother's house. In the evenings we visited with relatives, but our days were spent in Grandma's attic sorting through boxes of old pictures, mementos and junk. One box contained a newspaper clipping of my great-grandmother's wedding. The wedding picture next to it showed her in a long gown with a crown of orange blossoms in her hair. Another box contained that very crown. As we visited relatives, I took the family pictures with us which I had found in the attic. One by one they were identified, and we learned many stories about the lives of some of those persons.

Mom could remember as a child being driven along the main road by Smithtown (not far from Grandma's home). Members of Dad's family would point and say that there were "Baileys buried over there." With that bit of information we went to the old Smithtown cemetery but only found a lot of Smiths. Mom decided that maybe it was not Smithtown she was remembering but Riverhead, a town about 20 miles down the road. At the Riverhead archives in the local library was information on Rothermel, my great-grandmother's name. There were no Baileys in the Riverhead cemetery, so back we went to Smithtown.

At the historical department of the local Smithtown library was a little old man who seemed most anxious to talk, so Mom visited with him while I looked through the records. Almost immediately I opened the family history of Richard Smith, Esq., the founder of the town, and saw that my great-grandmother was listed as a contributor of this genealogical book. The information had been taken from her famly Bible. This helpful family history revealed to us how the Smiths and Baileys were related.

We were elated to discover that this book, recently reprinted by the Smithtown Historical Society, was for sale! A short time later, book in hand, we triumphantly returned to the Smithtown cemetery. Time was getting late, and still we found only Smiths, no Baileys. Then a young man came near, and we asked if he knew of any Baileys buried there. He led us to a remote part of the graveyard where there was a large monument inscribed with the Bailey name. There we found several generations of people for whom I had no previous records. Without this young man's help, we would not have found this part of the cemetery!

That night there was much information to record on my research sheets! Mom decided to telephone a man listed in the Richard Smith book (who lived nearby). When she introduced herself as Mildred Brooks Bailey, he seemed surprised but delighted to be of help to us. The next day he told us he felt as if he had been talking to a ghost since his sister's name had been Mildred Brooks. We discovered that we were distant cousins!

He recommended we visit the Mills Pond Cemetery, located at the top of a nearby hill. The death records of several Baileys had mentioned Mills Pond, and in two wills it was listed as the family estate. At the base of the hill was a large white frame house—obviously very old. It was next to a tiny pond which was almost hidden by huge trees.

The home had been recently purchased by an English couple who were interested in its past. They enjoyed reading the description of the property from the wills of John and Samuel Bailey (who were father and son). We walked through the house to the back porch, where a small stone path led to a little fenced-in cemetery. The stones of the pathway nearest the house were actually flat little headstones, marking the places of burial of the babies. They had not been buried up on the hill but down close to the house.

The cemetery on the hill contained the graves of people whose names were listed in my great-grandmother's Bible; the complete families of John Bailey, Samuel Bailey and the last generation to own the home, John Henry Bailey. We learned that the Bailey home had been in the family since before the Revolutionary War, and until the 1930s. That night, while pondering the new material I had added to the sheets, I noticed something odd. John Bailey, original owner of the Mills Pond house, had married Charity Smith. After she died he married her younger sister, Temperance. While John, Charity and their children were buried on the hill, Temperance was not. John's will stated that *all* his estate was to be left to his children, and that his wife, Temperance, could only have those articles which she had brought to the marriage.

Checking the Richard Smith book, I found the family of Charity and Temperance Smith, the children of gristmill owner Adam Smith who, in the late 1700s had lived about thirty miles from Mills Pond. The book also mentioned that many of the Smiths of that generation were buried in a family cemetery. I decided to obtain primary sources of information whenever possible (such as gravestones) to assure myself that what had been printed was correct. The next day the Historical Society in Smithtown directed us to the Adam Smith gristmill. They said the Frances Bacon home was once owned by Adam Smith. It was a large white two-story home nestled by an inlet near the bay and surrounded by acres of trees and flowers. The housekeeper there told us that the owner was away on vacation, and she had never heard of a cemetery nearby.

While returning to our car we noticed a young man walking down the path toward us. I asked if he had ever heard of a cemetery in the area. His answer was "No." He explained that he was the caretaker's son and that he had lived there for a long time. I told him of the book's claim that many Smiths had been buried in a family plot. He invited us to look over the grounds with him, and we were delighted to do so. While we walked he told us that as a child he had heard stories of ghosts. He did recall one story of a cemetery somewhere close by and had even heard rumors of boys going there on Halloween.

He took us over to an area overgrown with brambles and trees. It was such a dense tangle that we could not see inside. He seemed to think that this might be the place to which the story referred. We found a natural break in the tangle of shrubs that led into a huge, dark, damp, sylvan room, formed by the wall of bushes and canopy of trees. We were in Adam Smith's cemetery.

Temperance Smith Bailey's headstone was right in front of us. Not only was her headstone there with her vital statistics, but her immediate relatives were close by. Evidently, she had gone home to be with her mother and father, and she was buried with them instead of with her husband. Not far away were many more people (from the book) whose data could now be verified. This cemetery was so old that many of the grave markers dated into the late 1600s and were carved of wood. Because the area was so well protected from the weather, they were in fairly good condition. Returning to Smithtown we reported to the Historical Society that we had found the cemetery. Other than the mention in Richard Smith's genealogy book, they had no record of it.

The next day we drove on to Southold, a small town on the northern coast. We went first to the Historical Society's library. I had been there but a short time when I found an interesting Bailey genealogy. Having verified 250 years of Bailey names and dates at the gravesites, I felt I was in a good position to know whether this book held information on my family. It referred to a John Bailey and wife, Charity, and children with names the same as those of my ancestral family. In almost every case the dates of birth and death were off by no more than two or three years. The names fitted, the dates were very close, but the burial places were wrong for my family. There was no way that this could be the same group. Finding this information helped me to later correct a professional genealogist I employed who became entangled with *this* Bailey family, which was not mine.

Still at the Southold library I happened to open a book to a page that mentioned one of my known ancestors as having married a Youngs girl. Several generations of her people were documented in this genealogy, indicating that they had lived and died in Oyster Ponds, a settlement at the far eastern end of the island. Mom and I decided to drive to Oyster Ponds. Arriving at the local historical society, we asked the woman there if she knew of a 250-year-old Youngs cemetery. She remembered a very old cemetery and offered to take us there. We traveled down back streets and country roads to a little hill heavily shaded by dense woods, nestled in a very old area. The cemetery contained gravestones dating back to the late 1700s. Our Youngs were all there!

Our last Long Island trip included a visit with our very elderly Aunt Margaret, my great-grandmother's sister. She was the most difficult person I interviewed because of her great age and heavy German accent; yet she recalled events of her own childhood that helped me pin down information that pertained to *my* great-grandmother. I was able to learn of the family's place of origin in Germany, as well as to obtain four generations of family names. A short time after our interview, Aunt Margaret passed away.

Before leaving California I had written to my dad's Aunt Dorothy Bailey. She had become interested in genealogy when she had received the family Bible and records left to her by Dad's grandmother. She promised me she would have the records ready when I came. One day she felt inspired to go up in the attic to look for any genealogy I might want. Later, when we arrived at her home, she asked us to follow her to the attic. We were appalled to find it was black and charred. Aunt Dorothy told us that the attic had burned after she had followed an impression to retrieve the Bibles and other family papers.

Aunt Dorothy showed us the Bible of John and Samuel Bailey. It was the same Bible from which Great-grandmother had donated information for the Richard Smith genealogy. She also had information that added a few more generations on another King line.

Our last stop on the way home was Pollocksville, North Carolina, where the DuValls and Bryans had lived for generations. I interviewed several relatives, visited cemeteries and copied Bibles that took us back before the Civil War. Just when I thought I had every bit of information possible, an aunt remembered that Mom's grandparents and other close relatives were buried in an old family plot out in the country. A cousin remarked that it was thought strange that a tornado had leveled several acres of trees all around but had left the cemetery untouched!

Driving out into the country, we once more found a burial spot which was almost inaccessible! Here was a tiny family plot overgrown with brambles, thorned vines and huge trees. I could see into the plot but was not close enough to read the headstones without going into the vines and spider webs. I pushed my way in and copied down all the information. It was great! but how could I get out? While going in, the thorns had pointed away from me, but going out would be a different story. Just then a man rode by on a tractor and "just happened" to have a machete in his hand. Mom had him cut a way out for me.

After one more stop for some South Carolina information, Mother and I drove home to California. We had been gone almost five weeks. Almost every day I had been blessed with many new names, dates and places to add to my family history. With so little time available, the Lord (and I) had had to work fast. Books were opened to just the right page, people were in the right places at the right time, hidden cemeteries were revealed, my aunts lived long enough to give me vital information that only they had, and records were saved from fire and tornado.

I felt the Lord's guidance and inspiration each day, and I marveled as I watched information unfold. I am grateful for the experiences the Lord granted me in the summer of 1972.

IV

The Worldwide Family

FINDING PETER REPP

By Marlene Mays

Jagodnaja Poljana is located on the Volga River in the heartland of Russia. In 1765 it was a savage land which required hardworking, dependable people with a knowledge of farming who could settle it. The Tsarina of Russia, Catherine the Great, turned to the people she knew best, from her former homeland—Germany. She offered them free land, no taxes, freedom of religion and draft exemption. These promises were too good to miss, so her offer was enticing to many. My husband's Repp ancestors were among those pioneers who left Germany to resettle in Russia.

The Volga Germans' exodus from Russia began about 1882 when all the special privileges were revoked which had been granted to them. Most of these emigrants settled in the Palouse area of eastern Washington in the United States. News about the satisfying life in America soon reached friends and relatives in the Old Country, and a tide of emigration began which continued until World War I.

Peter Repp, my husband Don's grandfather, decided to search for a better life in a free country for his little family, which consisted of a wife and one child. He was able to emigrate to America and there make a comfortable living for them. His final home was in the state of Oregon in the Pacific Northwest where he died.

The family's history lay untouched for almost twenty-five years. Early one frantic morning the phone rang persistently. It was someone calling to say that a mutual friend was in spiritual need. She thought a drive together might lift her spirits. Would I like to come along and perhaps spend a few hours in the genealogical library?

Quickly I reviewed the forthcoming events of the day—a voice lesson, a doctor's appointment, two DAR committee meetings, etc.—the list went on and on. It seemed impossible to change my schedule at the last minute, but I felt compelled to try. A short prayer, and a few minutes later, I was headed across town with my dear friends. We had a wonderful time visiting together.

Arriving at the library without prior planning, I found myself at a loss, wandering about aimlessly searching, and for what, I wondered. My mother-in-law and her parents came to mind, but they were Germans, born in Russia, making research, I thought, almost impossible. Yet, I checked the index for some magic volume that might contain information to extend my husband's line. Mentioned was a book on German-Russians, which I hadn't examined, so I went to the shelf. As my hand reached for that book, I found myself taking a different one instead—one located right next to it. Mentally scolding myself for being so easily distracted, I opened the book and there was a query list of German-Russian names including the surnames of Lust and Repp, which are on my husband's maternal lines! They appeared to stand out boldly, making all other names dimmer by comparison.

Imagine my amazement! In all my years of research I had never run across these names. There they were and with information that a Mr. Lesser was interested in them, too. Oh, what luck! No, not luck, but one of the most spiritual experiences of my research career.

It was a few weeks before I wrote to Mr. Lesser regarding the Repp name, though a nagging urge to hurry constantly plagued me. My letter explained my husband's connection with the Repp name through his grandfather, Peter Repp, an emigrant from Russia.

Mr. Lesser's reply was prompt. Although he indicated his wife had been a Repp before their marriage, there seemed no apparent connection between our families. He recommended, however, that we contact the Prudential Insurance Company immediately as they were searching for heirs of one Peter Repp in order to settle his estate! Mr. Lesser gave me the policy number and details on this Peter Repp. He had lived on Cook Street in Portland, Oregon and would have been 100 years old if alive today. Zip! I went right up to Cloud Nine. I could hardly contain myself until my husband returned home to confirm the fact that his grandfather, Peter Repp, had indeed lived on Cook Street in Portland!

We contacted the insurance company. Although we had always believed that Peter was a simple man of little means, the policy had been purchased during the depression years. The insurance company asked us to supply them with proof of our relationship to Peter Repp. They would not commit themselves that a policy did, in fact, exist or that they were searching for the heirs. Two years and much correspondence later, we finally received a small portion of the estate of Grandfather Repp. It has been an exciting experience—one of those things that usually happens to "someone else."

When the time was right, this line, which had seemed impossible, opened in an incredible way. A short time later we learned of a German-Russian book authored and published by a distant cousin of my husband.* This man's background as a history major, plus his research and travels to Europe and Russia, enabled him to write of these people who emigrated from Russia and settled in eastern Washington. In interviews and pictures he told not only of their emigration to the United States but of their previous emigration from Germany to Russia and of the village which they helped settle there. One picture showed the village church and school which my husband's great-aunt still remembers and had told him about. This book is a timely and important research tool and is a great blessing to us.

I shudder to think of the blessings that might have been witheld if I had not put important appointments aside and listened with my heart to the needs of a friend. As is usually the case, my rewards were greater than I could possibly have imagined.

Pilgrims on the Earth, a German-Russian Chronicle by Richard D. Scheuerman.

FUN ON AN ANCESTRAL CHASE

By Irene Ricks

For a long time I had been interested in genealogical research but just didn't feel that I had the time. My excuse was that such people get so involved they seem to have time for nothing else. I was interested in a variety of things, not only my ancestors. Another obstacle in my way was that I didn't know what to do or where to start. I once had an orientation tour at a large genealogical library, but after the tour I felt as though I was in the middle of the deep blue sea and didn't know how to swim!

The day came when I gathered together what courage I had to try again. After fumbling around on my own a few hours I was advised to go to the British section of the library. I was bewildered as I looked at the rows of books and files of films. I just couldn't believe that any of my ancestors' names were in there. I vy Morris of the British section of the library came to my rescue. She looked at my charts and suggested that I search the 1851 census of St. Albans, for my Grandfather Warwick, on Mother's side of the family. Ivy said that the name Warwick should be easy for a beginner to work on because it was not as common as some of the other names on my chart.

In this way I was introduced to the procedure of searching census records. After many hours of fruitless effort I said to myself: "This isn't for me. I've got to have more to show for my time than this." Then suddenly, there appeared on the microfilm screen the names of my great-great-grandparents! There they were—living right in St. Albans, Hertfordshire, on Fishpool Street. The year was 1851. I could hardly believe my eyes. Another turn of the film, and I beheld the family of my great-grandparents and a three-year-old boy who subsequently became my grandfather. No longer were they just names on a pedigree chart! Now time had turned back more than a century, and I was in a dream world, visiting St. Albans, going along Fishpool Street, walking by the Old Mill and meeting the people in their homes!

The more I researched in and about St. Albans the more I wished to visit that historic town. Gradually the wish became an over-whelming desire to go to England, not just to sightsee and visit living relatives, but to examine records and visit the places where my ancestors had once lived.

I made the trip with my brother's wife, Elda Urry Hailes, whose Urry ancestors, like my Hailes ones, had come from the Isle of Wight. Before we left I visited with Ben Bloxham, an authority on English genealogical research. He had just returned from two years of graduate work in England and was very helpful, telling me just what to do when I arrived in London. He warned me to be prepared and not to go to England to do research without the faintest notion of where to start, as many people did. In a small notebook I listed the names and addresses of eleven places I must visit:

1. Public Record Office (known as the PRO)
    Chancery Lane

2. Society of Genealogists
    37 Harrington Gardens
    London SW7

3. St.Catherine's House

4. British Museum

5. H.M.S.O. (Her Majesty's Stationery Office)

6. Guildhall Library
    Basinghall Street, London

7. Hertfordshire County Record Office
    County Hall, Hertford

8. Hampshire Record Office
    20 Southgate Street, Winchester

9. Portsmouth City Record Office
    Buildhall, Portsmouth

10. Isle of Wight County Record Office
    26 Hillside, Newport

11. Nottinghamshire Record Office
    County House, High Pavement, Nottingham

12. Essex Record Office
    County Hall, Chelmsford

All of these places were carefully listed in a small notebook which I carried in my bag along with my wallet, passport, travelers checks, and Britrail pass.

We arrived in England at Gatwick airport at 4:30 a.m. A couple came up to us and introduced themselves as Wendell and Muriel

Rawlings. They had been on the same plane and had learned of our purpose. Not knowing what to do except visit cemeteries, they asked if I would help them. I explained that I was a rank beginner myself, but that I had learned that erosion, decay and neglect in old cemeteries in England made them a less-than-desirable source of information. I offered to share with the Rawlings the information in my notebook, the one thing that gave me courage and confidence. We reviewed my notes as we rode together into London on the train.

The four of us spent the next three days riding the Underground, the famous red London double-deck buses, and the shiny black taxis to the Public Record Office, St. Catherine's House, the Guildhall Library, Her Majesty's Stationery Office, the Genealogical Society, and the British Museum. It was all exciting and very rewarding, much more fun than merely sightseeing. In fact, our adventures made ordinary sightseeing dull by comparison. From the Genealogical Society we purchased excellent maps of the counties in which we wanted to research.

All four of us were now full of enthusiasm and ready to venture forth to our various counties. The Rawlings went their way while Elda and I proceeded to the town of St. Albans, which is not far from London. There we went to church as it was Sunday. As people talked to us after the meeting we told them of our plans to do genealogical research. Someone said, "You must meet Mister Mount. He has done much research in Hertfordshire and will be able to help you."

When we met him, we had the feeling that we had found a real friend. He was very enthusiastic and volunteered to help us look for our Halsey and Warwick names—names he had not worked on in his fifty years of research in Hertfordshire. I had a feeling of anticipation that sometimes comes with listening to the still small voice of the Spirit. I knew we had been prompted to go to St. Albans that Sunday afternoon.

The next morning we met Mister Mount in the Hertford Record Office. Though he had only arrived a few minutes before us, he had already written down five marriages he had found! I looked at them, and saw the names of Daniel Halsey and Lucy How, married 26 October 1806. "My great-great-grandparents!" I exclaimed with emotion, and it seemed as if I could hear the angels singing,

"Hallelujah! Hallelujah!" Thus the fun of ancestor-hunting started. During the day we found the Halseys' ten children. Our excitement knew no bounds. The next several days proved just as fascinating as we unraveled more family history.

Our itinerary next took us to the home of Geoffrey and Aubrey Clench in Southampton, Hampshire. They had hundreds of marriages and baptisms on file in their home, and the first night there we found John Hurst married to Mary Greenaway; John Hurst, Sr., married to Sarah Gover; and William Greenaway married to Elizabeth Wilson, my second and third great-grandparents. The next day we went to the record office in Portsmouth. On the way there I said I had a feeling that we were going to make a discovery of some importance, and indeed we did! Joseph Hurst married to Margaret Bennett! My father had been told that Joseph Hurst married Margaret Hurst, who was supposed to be a cousin. This had been a great stumbling-block for many years, but now that knot had been unraveled. It opened up the discovery that John Bennett married Jane Bartley and that William Bartley married Sarah Atkins. Again my heart sang as we discovered names of great-great-grandparents.

While in Portsmouth I had the added excitement of visiting my own birthplace. It was near the birthplace of Charles Dickens. The door to his home had a big bronze plaque inscribed, "The birthplace of Charles Dickens." The inscription on the door of my birthplace was merely, "61 Byerly Road."

Our next point of interest was the Isle of Wight. My inherited seafaring blood stirred within me as we sailed to that beautiful island. I knew that my ancestors had been in the Royal Navy, and I hoped to find out more about them. We found our way to the record office in Newport. As we came to the door we paused, not quite sure it was the right place, but the door swung open and a cheerful voice said: "Yes, this is the record office. What can we do to help you?"

I explained that I was looking for Williams and Hailes names, and Elda said she was looking for Urry names. "Oh, great!" came the reply, "We just finished researching Urry names, and we have a list of Urry marriages since 1550."

"May I copy them?" asked Elda, almost afraid to breathe.

"We will just xerox them for you," was the answer. And so for a few pence Elda got a copy of 256 Urry marriages to add to her family data. Again our hearts were singing.

While on the Isle of Wight we had another delightful experience. We went to the Whippingham Parish, where we found the vicar to be very kind and cooperative. In fact, he gave us unrestricted access to a safe in which all the records were kept. The parish itself had special interest for us because Elda's great-great-grandmother had been married there. Incidentally we learned when the vicar took us on a tour around the building that one of Queen Victoria's daughters had been married there.f

We next visited the record office in Winchester and found some wills that gave us much interesting information about the families of our great-grandparents. When we went to lunch we learned that we were within a stone's throw of King Arthur's original roundtable area. Of course, we had to go there and take pictures.

We left King Arthur's land to see Robin Hood's; Nottingham was to be our last stop. Our month was coming to an end all too quickly. Some English cousins went with us and had their first experience with record searching at the Nottingham record office. They enjoyed it as much as we did, all four of us writing names as fast as we could write. They were amazed to find out how easy it was to find the names for our family tree. In just a few hours we found ancestors dating back to 1710. Our cousins volunteered to go on with the search because they realized that we had merely made a good start in the limited time we had been together.

There is something about genealogical research that makes you want to share the excitement of discovery with your family and friends. We kept sending letters and cards regularly, but we could hardly wait to tell them in person about our success. We were eager to tell our good friend Ben Bloxham about our good fortune and how we had profited through his expert guidance. The Rawlings flew home on the same plane with us, and they also were enthusiastic and grateful for their experience.

Mister Bloxham put it very well when he said to us: "This proves that you have the Lord on your side, and if you have courage to go forth with enthusiasm, you can have success in genealogical research—even if you are just a beginner."

MY SWEDISH CONNECTION

By George E. Larsson

In 1951 I was single and living in New Haven, Connecticut. I had saved some money, so I decided to quit my job and take a trip to Europe for sightseeing and to try to find my relatives in Sweden.

My father, Martin Larsson, came to the United States in 1895 with his father and mother, when he was five years old. They settled in Cambridge, Massachusetts. When my father grew up and started his own family, he bought a house in nearby West Newton. My grandmother and grandfather had died before 1927, and we only had the address of my grandfather's sister, Ida Karlsson, in Vastervik, Sweden. No correspondence had taken place since 1940 when my father sent my high school graduation picture along with a letter, but received no reply.

When I arrived at Stockholm, I took a train to Vastervik arriving about the middle of the day. It was a very pleasant small town, and I walked around until I found a family rooming house and took a room for the night. I then went to the street address that I had, but found no one there who knew the name of Ida Karlsson or my grandfather, Lars Larsson. My Swedish was rather primitive, and they knew no English, so communication was difficult.

As I continued to walk around the town, I came upon a small police station, so I went in and inquired about Ida Karlsson. Fortunately, several of the policemen knew some English, and they were all extremely friendly. They asked me to get in the police car, and we went back to the address where they had a long talk with the residents. Then we went back to the station where they made several telephone calls. Finally, they took me to a house outside of the town where a family came out to greet me; a middle-aged mother and father and two teenage daughters. They shook my hand, embraced me and invited me inside, and the policemen went away.

One of the girls, Ulla, who was sixteen years old, was quite a scholar. She spoke English quite well and also knew German, French and some Spanish. She told me her father's name was Ville Lonnberg and that her mother, Karin, was a daughter of Ida Karlsson, Karin being the youngest of twelve children. She said Ida had died in the early 1930s which seemed to fit in with the little information that I had. I found myself wondering if these were really the right relatives since there was a possibility there could have been more than one Ida Karlsson.

My doubt was soon dispelled when they took me into the living room and there hanging on the wall was my graduation picture! Now I knew I was in the right place! The Karlsson family had received the letter and the picture, but since Ida had died, there was no one left who personally knew any of the relatives who had gone to America. In time, the 1940 letter and other correspondence had been misplaced or lost. Of the twelve children, the picture was given to Karin, the youngest, but all that was known was that this was a relative in the United States. They knew no names, addresses or the exact relationship. Strangely enough, I had found the one home in all of Sweden that could have my graduation picture on the wall! It was conclusive evidence of their American connection and my Swedish connection!

I spent a pleasant three weeks in Vastervik and eventually met more than fifty other people who were my cousins and their families. I was invited to many parties and social activities, some of which were in honor of me, their new-found American relative.

A TONGAN TALE

By Sau Fangupo Manusina

In America when many young people reach eighteen years of age, they feel they are "free to go." In Tonga this is not true. We are taught to never go away from your family, for each family member is loved and respected. The generations learn to help one another and are usually very happy living together.

When I was a little boy about six years old, I went with my parents to the "bushes." Because we lived in town, we had to travel about five miles to our sixteen-acre farming area where we could plant and grow our food: taro and tapioca, bananas, mangoes and papayas, pineapples, and other delicious things to eat. We worked together to grow our food.

When young people are old enough, they bring their "dates" home to become friends with the family. Regular dating usually does not take place until after teen years, often until twenty-one. Single adults live at home until they are married. A wedding is a time of great celebration for everyone and a luau is prepared with pig, fish, chicken, and many other delicious things to eat. All the relatives and friends from the islands are invited to come. The party in honor of the happy couple usually lasts several hours, and everyone has a wonderful time.

Older people are much respected by the younger members of the household. Because of their age and experience, they are very wise and give good counsel. When the father of the family is old and unable to care for his family, the child will take care of his parents. Sometimes the children live with the grandparents. We used to sleep in the same room, and my parents and grandparents would tell stories of long ago. That is how Tongan history was passed down through the generations. Tongan customs and culture are also taught in the schools.

I remember a very happy time when I was twelve years old. Our family visited my father's parents, 'Aisea (Isaiah) Pukavahe and Maile Tapaita Fangupo on the island of Vavau. (He came from Falehau and she from Utungake on Vavau, smaller Tongan islands.) We sat around and told many stories, and I learned much about the history and genealogy of our people. The large main island of Tonga is surrounded by almost two hundred smaller ones. Tonga has one king who rules over all the islands.

My mother's parents, Filimone and Meleti Matakaionga, were from Vaini on the island of Tongatapu in Tonga. They had a family of seven children. One day a big ship came to visit the island and brought some strange disease. Many Tongan people died, and it was very sad. Grandfather Filimone died at age 37, the same day as his two daughters, Mele and Olivia. I did not know them for this happened many years ago.

When someone dies, relatives come, even from long distances. The deceased remains at home so everyone can come to pay their last respects. The night before the funeral everyone will be awake all night visiting with the relatives, some of whom they have not seen for a long time. After the funeral the body is taken to be buried in the village graveyard.

Mosese (Moses) Fangupo came from Utungake on the island of Vavau in Tonga. Sioana Ungatea Havea Fangupo was born in Kolomotua on Tongatapu island. They were my father's mother's parents. My Great-grandmother Fangupo's genealogy extends back into royalty, hundreds of years, back to the year 950. Kings Tokemoana I, II and III reigned in the 1700s, Havea I and II in the 1300s and Oho Eitu about 950, first king of Tonga. Great-grandmother's ancestors were all Tongan except for one Samoan grandmother who lived four hundred years ago, about 1568.

Grandfather Mosese was a remarkable man. He was over seven feet tall. He and his wife, Sioana, were Methodists, and he used to work for the church. Grandfather lived to be about 100 years old. When he died, he still had all his teeth and hair. Their home was made from the coconut trees. The roof was made from the leaves and the rest of the tree was used for the walls. They fished and grew many fruits and other commodities to sell at market. They wove their own mats, made beautiful cloth out of leaves and grasses and other necessary items. These were all part of their culture and are now part of our heritage.

My father, Timote Manusina Pukavahe, was born in Falehau, Niua-Toputapu, and raised in Vavau, another small island in Tonga. His family members are very large in stature, and he was seven feet tall. When my father was a volunteer soldier in the Tongan army, he came to the larger island of Tonga and during the time of World War II, and met my mother, 'Ilaisaane Matakatongo. They were married and had nine children: Moses, Pisila, Uata, Kina, Alisis, Oualeni, Toa, Katea, and I am the youngest, Sau Fangupo Manusina. We have been raised on the larger island of Tonga.

SAU FANGUPO MANUSINA

In Tonga today there are many changes. There are many small villages and each village has elementary, junior high and high schools as wells as various churches. There are about twenty high schools on the main island. The homes and facilities are more modern. There are many different religions in the islands: Methodists, Catholics, Baptists, Seven-Day Adventists and Mormons.

Many Tongan people now keep family records. The written genealogy is called "Tohihohoki." The government also keeps vital records.

I, Sau, am now married to a beautiful bride, Mele Kinikini. When we have children, we will tell them about the history and genealogy of our Tongan people. We will teach our descendants, "You never go away from your family."

DISCOVERING HEIDI'S HOMELAND
By Bernice Lorraine Dealer

After enjoying a day in picturesque Innsbruck, my daughter, Diane, and I boarded the "Schnellzugg" for eastern Switzerland and the city of Chur, an old Roman trade city. The fast train's large picture windows afforded us a breathtaking panorama of the peaceful Austrian countryside. Colorful chalets, always part of the changing scene, clung to the hillsides and surrounded each village church where steeple domes of brightly-tinted hues shone in the sun. Rivers dashed down through the steep mountain slopes and over rocks and hills to the valley below. We were ecstatic over so much beauty!

Looking back, I remembered when Diane was growing up, I had found among a quaint collection of books a worn and faded-green copy of "Heidi" by Johanna Spyri. Diane never tired of hearing the beautiful story of the little girl who lived with her kindly grandfather in a hut in the Alps of Switzerland. She used to sit curled up in our large overstuffed chair, reading it over and over, and loving it, and dreaming that some day she might visit this far away land. As a little girl, I had also dreamed of going to Switzerland. My mother had told me that her grandparents were Swiss, and that many of our ancestors had come from there. One of the most special (to me) was my great-grandmother, Sara Burn, who had come to America with her family in the early 1800s, and settled in Ohio. She married her childhood sweetheart, Christian Germann, and raised a family. He became a Christian minister, moved to Indiana, and . . . .

My thoughts were interrupted by a conductor at the far end of the coach calling out the next station: "Sargons! Sargons!" This came moments before the tᵣ in stopped. We almost missed the station but the man in the next seat reminded us by saying, "Aren't you going to Chur? Then you must change trains here." Hurriedly, we grabbed our luggage and jumped off just as the train started to pull out.

A number of people thronged the small station for snacks, sundries and the latest newspaper. A regiment of uniformed Swiss soldiers passed by. After a long wait, we boarded a slower train to Chur. The countryside slowly changed as we wended our way down through the verdant valleys. A few ancient fortresses of crumbling stone stood sentry on the hillsides. The movement of the train lulled me back to thoughts of "Heidi," and I remembered again the inspiring influence of that little old book. Diane's curiosity about Switzerland took her to other sources. After reading a beautifully illustrated article in the *National Geographic* she wrote a letter of thanks to the Swiss authorities.

I recalled that Diane enjoyed learning about the friendly, quaintly-dressed villagers of Dorfli, Bad Ragaz and Maienfeld, bustling about, fulfilling their lives in their chalets, shops or attending the village church. She loved to imagine the breathtaking beauty of the Falknis Berg "where the sun set fire to the mountains" and the Casaplana "where the eagle soared among the crags." She would picture in her mind the nimble white goats and gentle brown cows grazing on the slopes. Since childhood Diane and I both had treasured our dreams of this intriguing land.

After years of research into our Burn and Germann families, we finally did learn their place of origin, the Alpine village of Adelboden in Canton Bern. Part of our dreams had come true in a memorable week two years previously when we gathered new relatives and old records. Now it was time to bring all our dreams to reality! The parish registers and a history of Adelboden revealed the Burn and Germann families extended back to the fifteenth century in Frutigen and Adelboden. There we found the parents of Great-grandmother Sara, Johannes Germann and Anna "Nanette" Christina Heinrich, the daughter of Pastor Lucas and Christina Roffler Heinrich of Igis, Canton of Graubunden, Switzerland. Then and there Diane and I decided we would also find a way to visit the homeland of our Heinrich ancestors.

Now, as the train continued on, it was almost unbelievable when we actually saw the stations of Bad Ragatz and Maienfeld. We felt as if we were stepping back into the storybook pages of "Heidi."

We arrived at Chur in the early evening. We carried our bags to the nearest phone booth and called Frau Schmid whom we had previously written. She spoke only German so she referred us to Frau Vivien Hemmi who spoke English. This lady was so gracious, inviting us to stay with them. She sent her husband, Fred, and son, Alan, to meet us at the station. Soon we were riding up the mountain to their chalet where Vivien was waiting. Right away it seemed as if we had always known them. They made us feel so welcome.

After supper dishes were over, we went into the living room. Fred was seated at a table in the corner poring over a large pedigree chart. He had a desire to begin working on genealogy, he said, but did not know how to begin. Relatives had given him records on several occasions, and now he was in the process of trying to put them in order on the chart. It was slow going. Diane said, "May I help? I am a genealogist." Fred brightened.

When we walked over to see his records, we almost fainted! There were Eggers, Schranzs, Klopfensteins and many other familiar names from Adelboden and Frutigen! By the time we compared our genealogies, we were able to give Fred twelve new generations on his direct lines! We were really cousins! We had gone half-way around the world to work on Great-grandmother Sara's mother's family, and we had found these cousins on her father's lines. What a surprise! Fred was thrilled with the new information and began copying names as fast as he could.

While we stayed in their mountain chalet, Vivien and Fred were wonderful to us. Vivien even brought hot water bottles to our beds on those chilly fall nights near the top of the mountain. The food they prepared for us was delicious! Fred was a baker in the public schools in Chur. They helped us with our genealogy by phoning several pastors (who spoke only German) for information about our families.

Fred kindly drove the winding roads to the old village of Igis where we obtained one of the ancient land books replete with "Heinrichs." However, no Anna or "Nanette" was listed. It did contain a number of familiar surnames but few dates of any consequence, and gave a historical picture of the village landowners. One day Fred and Vivien took us to meet some of the Heinrich and Roffler descendants. One, Herr Naser, let us copy his Heinrich family chart which extended back several generations.

Another day we took bus, train, and finally a taxi to the Gemeindehaus in the newer town of Igis. They had recently moved, and the books were stored in the bottom shelf of an old cabinet in a busy office. Diane showed the officer in charge her permission-visa from the Canton police, but he waved it aside and explained they were preparing for an important civic conference in the adjoining office. When he learned we had come so far, he was very kind and shared his corner desk with us. We promised to be quiet and not bother anyone. (Later he let us make copies and even took an interest and helped us translate a few words of the old script.)

Finally they began their conference in the next room. We sat down at the desk with one of the large parish registers. Oh, how we prayed to be able to read the old script. Carefully, we turned the precious pages until a faintly written date of 1771 appeared to stand out from all the others. Then we saw the marriage record of Pastor "Lutzy" and Christina Roffler Heinrich, the parents of Christina Heinrich. As we turned forward in the book to obtain the christening records of their children, we discovered that our own Pastor Heinrich had filled in the entries with his own beautiful script. We found the records of his parents, Baltz (Balthazar) and Ursula Ladner Heinrich, and continued to search for additional relatives. Before we knew it, our day was gone. Regretfully, we closed the large old book. We also leafed through a smaller book of earlier vintage written in a much more difficult old script, but it was impossible to decipher in the few moments we had left. We wished for more time, but it was gone, so we returned to the Hemmi's chalet to make preparations for the journey home.

That night Herr Schmid came by and helped us read some of the difficult place names in the records written in the old German script. We learned that the Rofflers had come from Fideris, a nearby village in the Prattigau valley (another reminder of "Heidi"). If only there had been more time to visit each hallowed place.

The morning we left for America it was pouring rain as we slowly made our way down the mountainside. We felt so sad to leave our new cousins, the Hemmis, and our Heinrich homeland. As we reviewed every happening, we remembered how we had prayed for the way to be opened to obtain the records in Igis, that the pastors would understand how important it was for us to find our ancestral family. We also needed to be able to read the difficult script, and finally, to obtain a permission-visa from the Canton police to allow us to work in the records. It was wonderful how all these things came about. We discovered living relatives and the maternal family of Great-grandmother Sara, as well as extending her ancestral lines for several generations.

After we returned home letters soon began flying back and forth to Malix, Igis, Fideris and other Swiss villages. The capstone of this exciting research came when we received in the mail a copy of the old parish register from our cousin Vivien Hemmi. She had gained permission to copy the whole book which began in the 1600s. Later, she sent a record from the village of Fideris. Meanwhile, we found in the archives in Salt Lake City seventeen additional direct-line families to be added to the genealogy of Fred Hemmi!

Two years later the Hemmis and Muriel Schmid visited us in America. Those wonderful people had driven many kilometers to gather information for us. They brought with them a slide presentation of some of the villages and churches in Switzerland where Pastor Heinrich had preached. (These pictures have since been added to a biographical history of the Heinrich family.) It was wonderful just like stepping back in time. The Hemmis invited my grandson, Stephen, to live with them and attend school for a term.

He loved it and learned to speak German, a little French and Hoke-Deutsch. It was amazing how, with the Lord's help, everything had worked out andour dreams had come true!

Just think, all of these things came to pass because I was inspired to pick up an old faded copy of "Heidi."

TURKISH QUILTMAKER'S FAMILY
By Sule Cakmak

My great-grandfather was born in Constantinople (Istanbul), Turkey around the year 1859. When he grew up, he worked and lived in the royal palace as the royal quiltmaker to the Sultan. The Yorgan or Turkish quilts he designed were or silk or satin, embroidered or outlined with beautiful designs and stuffed with cotton or unsheared wool. They were big, bulky, and warm for the freezing below-zero winters. My great-grandfather was a skilled artisan, and he became quite wealthy. He lived in the palace until he was about forty years old, and then moved himself and his family to Trabzon which is located in the north of Turkey.

My grandfather was born in Trabzon in a little village called Macka. (Many of the paternal side of my family live there today. A typical dwelling in that village still has stables to house the animals on the first level and living quarters on the second and third floors.) While living in Trabzon they bought thousands of acres of land and started farming. They raised filbert nuts for oil, cooking and eating. My grandfather married a woman from Trabzon and had three sons. He met a widow later whose husband had died during a war and married her as well. My father was born to this lady so she was my grandmother. (In those days during the rule of the Sultan, Islamic law controlled the main block of government laws, so men were allowed to have more than one wife.) When Grandfather's first wife died, he took Grandmother and all four of the children and moved to Ankara, where he started a chain of notions stores, going back to the business of his father.

After working with his father and brothers in the family business, my father decided that he would like to pursue a career in medicine. He completed his schooling at the University of Ankara in Turkey and came to the United States to do his internship in Baltimore, Maryland, bringing his family. After living in this country from 1958 to 1963 he moved my brother, two sisters and myself to Turkey where we lived for three years. Then we returned to the United States and have been here ever since.

When my grandfather passed away in 1962, we returned to Turkey, because my grandmother was now alone. Even though my uncles were there, my father still felt a duty to his mother. After a time he brought her back to America and cared for her. Grandmother was bedridden for four years before she died at age 99. Though caring for her was difficult, my parents never considered putting her in a rest home. I am sure when I grow older, my family will take care of me in the same Turkish tradition. My paternal great-grandmother died in Istanbul at age 110. I visited her grave and have seen her tombstone. In Turkey a cemetery is a very sacred place.

Islam is the main religion in our country. Our people are faithful Moslems who follow Mohammed as well as other Old Testament prophets. The family is the main pillar of life and living in Turkey. Everything is done for the good of the whole family. The respect shown toward our elders and the emphasis that is put on their opinions is tremendous! I feel this attitude affects the entire style of living in the country. In some rural areas of Turkey there are two or three generations of a family that live in the same dwelling. The grandfather or oldest living relative is patriarch, or occasionally matriarch, of the family, governing and ruling the other members' lives; not as a dictatorship, but with a lot of value and respect shown for their opinions. Because exact genealogical records are not kept in Turkey, the family histories are transmitted orally from generation to generation.

We now have a second generation of my family growing up in the United States. We will probably continue living in this country, but I doubt that the connection we have with our mother country will ever be broken. My side of the family and all of my husband's relatives as well are still living in Turkey. One of my sisters recently married and is now living in Istanbul with no plans of returning to this country, but only time will tell.

Even today in Turkey, every home uses the traditional Yorgan or Turkish quilt. One of my uncles owns a quiltmaking store in Ankara, and only a street away my cousin also keeps such a shop of quilts but for sentimental reasons. Here in America I enjoy my Turkish Yorgan. Its soft warmth and beauty brings back pleasant memories of family and homeland. I am proud to be a member of a Turkish quiltmaker's family.

"WORLDLY" FAMILY TOGETHERNESS
By Carol A. Pooley

Summers on the beach at Lake Michigan most influenced me to establish my life goal of family togetherness. Unexpectedly, a visit to a library in Adelaide, Australia helped me achieve this.

Often on summer weekends during my childhood, all the cousins, aunts, uncles and grandparents assembled at the beach. We cousins played together all day in the sand and water while the grownups swam, sunned and took long walks along the shore. We were invited to accompany them. We walked along in twos and threes and talked and laughed together. The groups were fluid; we would walk with one, then skip back to join another, or run forward to slip our hand into that of another loved one. In the evening, after jointly preparing and consuming a feast at the cottage, we carried blankets down to the beach, gathered wood and built a bonfire. We sang together while the sun set and the moon rose, accompanied by the sound of waves surging to and from the shore.

Many years later when time, job opportunities and life tragedies had separated us, I wanted more than anything else to have my immediate family unified. Our five children are married, and we have twelve grandchildren. None live nearer than 800 miles, but frequent letters and visits have helped to keep us close. I felt our children would have a greater sense of unity if they knew from whom they came.

Our larger family is scattered (mostly) throughout the United States, but I live in Nova Scotia in Eastern Canada with My English-born husband, John Pooley. He is a professor, and I am an administrator at Dalhousie University. I also do some research and writing. This interest, combined with my desire to know more about my ancestral family, made me want to do genealogical research. I especially wanted to know more about my paternal grandmother, Ethel Margaret Dibdin Moore, and her family, the Dibdins. When I was growing up, I had a wonderful step-grandmother, Gerda Moore, whom I dearly loved, but I always wanted to know about the English lady who had gone away when my father was a teenager. There was a divorce. I never saw my grandmother, and no one would say much about her except that she couldn't adjust to middle-class life in America. I thought if I knew more about her background, I could better understand why she left.

Home and work obligations stood in the way of my research until last year, when John was on a year-long around-the-world study leave from the university. Genealogy filled my need to find a research interest to occupy my time during our sojourn in various places in the United States, England and Australia. In Australia I found the longed-for information about Grandmother Dibdin's family.

While in Perth, I spent hours looking for my family in the university library. My Uncle Charles Moore had started a family tree, and after Uncle died, Dad gave it to me because of my interest in genealogy. He had listed my great-grandfather's name as William James Dibdin who married Margaret Aglio. A trip to Somerset House corrected that error. By checking the records under the wife's name, I found that the names were actually William *Joseph* Dibden who married *Marion* Aglio. I had been told that Great-grandfather Dibdin was a well-known chemist. Through him we were believed to be related to Charles Dibdin and his sons, Charles and Thomas, a family of minor English actors, playwrights and theater managers. At the library I looked in the reference section and found them listed in some biographical dictionaries. Most of the biographies included the names of wives, but my second great-grandfather's did not. I had learned his name, Thomas Robert Coleman Dibdin, from my great-grandparent's marriage certificate, which I ordered from Somerset (now St. Catherine's House) during a stopover in London. I thought I needed to go back there to find my great-great-grand*mother's* name, as well as a positive connection to the playwrights. I despaired of this, however, as we did not plan to stop in London again.

My research in Perth was interrupted when we were invited on a lecture tour to Tasmania and eastern Australia which included a stop at Adelaide. We stayed with our host couple. While the men spent days at the university, the wife was left to entertain me. More to help her out, I told her I would enjoy visiting the state library to do some genealogical research.

At the library when I asked at the genealogy section about materials relating to England, the librarian replied that they only had information about Australian immigrants. Disappointed, I decided to go upstairs and explore the reference room. After browsing more than an hour, to my amazement I discovered one whole floor-to-ceiling section, and half of another, filled with typed-bound copies of parish registers: baptism, burial and marriage records of various churches of London, England which extended back to the 1500s! Excitedly, I paged through them one by one. Hours later I had nearly reached the bottom of the section when I found the marriage record of Thomas Robert Coleman Dibdin and Ann Alice Jones, my great-great-grandparents! Later I also found the record of this grandfather's birth which named *his* father, Thomas John Dibdin! He *was* one of the sons in the family of theater people! Halfway around the world from my home, I proved the old family story to be true!

I did return to London after all and heard about the Library of the Society of Genealogists. In their archives they had a long, yellowing Dibdin family chart which resembled an old scroll. The information was not all complete nor correct. I had learned that Thomas Dibdin was the father of Charles, the original playwright. Thomas was the church clerk in Holy Rood Church in Southampton, so I went to the records of that church and there I found the dates of all of Charles Dibdin's siblings. My own research, using the original church records, had confirmed and completed the Dibdin genealogy back to the early 1700s.

On our way home we visited all our children, some siblings, uncles, aunts and parents. When we shared our experiences, they were received with awe and excitement. Without exception, each individual has wanted to know more. This focus on our ancestors has somehow made the physical distance between us unimportant. We may not have summers together on the beach, but we are achieving family togetherness.

V

The Eternal Family

JUDY O. BURTON

SACRIFICES UNDERSTOOD
By Judy O. Burton

In this busy, up-to-date world, I find it hard to turn my thoughts to my forefathers. Several years ago, however, I did have a special experience about my ancestors that brought great meaning to my life. I was given a history of my grandmother, Hannah Merilda Crane Rindlisbacher. I never knew her for she died many years before I was born. As I read her story, I was amazed because of something which had recently happened to me.

My husband, Fred, and I were the parents of four normal, healthy children: Kristi, Cheri, Brian and Jamie. I had no problems with any of my pregnancies or the births of these children. Then I became pregnant for the fifth time, but after three months I had a miscarriage. I felt so disappointed, but I soon got over it. I knew that God has a plan for each of us, and I had the assurance that everything would be all right. Later, with relatively few problems, I did have a fifth baby, Scott. When I became pregnant again, I experienced mixed emotions. I made up my mind, however, to be excited about a sixth child. We all looked forward to the coming event. I was well into the fourth month of my pregnancy when problems arose, and I suffered another miscarriage. Conditions were very difficult, but I was in the hospital and received the best of care. Eventually, all turned out well.

Then, my grandmother, Hannah Merilda's story touched my life. I learned that her mother, Hannah Roseannah Butterfield Crane, died at age 31 after suffering a miscarriage and a subsequent stroke. Hannah Merilda was only thirteen at the time. (She had a very trying life for her father died two years later.) As I read on, I discovered that Grandmother Rindlisbacher, when in her thirties, died in the same way when her daughter, Leone, was twelve. Leone became my own mother. At the time of my last miscarriage, I was also in my early thirties, and my daughter, Kristi, like Leone and Hannah, was around twelve! Because of my own experience, I felt that I understood so much more about my grandmothers' lives than the few words I had read in the history. I appreciated it so much. I feel my grandmothers wanted me to know that they understood and cared. I know that that history came to me just when I needed it. I look forward to meeting and embracing my grandmothers one day.

I have learned that the heart can turn in understanding to my forefathers (and foremothers)! Our own lives can be enriched with understanding as we read of their lives and see similarities to our own. These women did not have the conveniences of our busy world, nor did they have the medical help we do, but my grandmothers were *real* people just like me! They had their own thoughts, feelings and love for husbands and children, just as I do for mine.

We love our children and enjoy watching them grow, learn and struggle to succeed. They bring joy to our lives. Hopefully, they won't have to experience the hardships my mother and grandmothers had to endure. I am grateful to be here to raise my children. If I had it to do over again, I would still choose to have every one.

RECOGNIZED ASSISTANCE

By Velma M. Lupton Mason

I am not a learned genealogist, but I have had a very fascinating time since 1976. My driven, almost religious search has led me through uncanny circumstances, to people who have helped me, especially on the research of my mother's family, the Ballards.

I always knew I had descended from William Bradford of Plymouth Colony. This awareness somehow stimulated me to find other lineage connections. I remembered my grandfather, Lloyd Ballard, saying about some inappropriate action, "A lady does not act like that. Never forget that you are a Ballard." This was something he felt I should live up to.

Before she died thirty-eight years ago, Mother gave me my piano. The bench contained only my music I thought. Instead I found there a well-worn family Bible which, for some reason, I decided to keep. It had been signed by Joseph Ballard, but very little vital information was recorded there. Then among my music I found a typed outline on my Bradford and Lamb families, done by my Grandmother Morgan. But the date of her marriage to Giles Morgan was not there! Now that I have become interested in my ancestral families, it does not seem possible that my parents and my grandfather never confided any information about their families. They probably thought it was of no concern to children.

Years later when I applied for a passport, I discovered I did not have proof of my birth. I needed to have another look at that Bible! To my disappointment, I found that the Ballard information had been removed, but another member of the family supplied it. About this time I became interested in joining the N.S.D.A.R. (National Society of Daughters of the American Revolution). My obsession to know my family history developed into a drive I could not ignore. This led me to a second cousin I had never known existed. They knew nothing of me. Although my brother was not interested, his wife had found some family books that belonged to my parents, and fortunately, she had kept them.

In my search I visited a Baptist church in Blossburg, Pennsylvania. The minister was very apologetic as he explained that a former minister had burned all the old records. He went on to tell me of an unusual old woman about eighty-five years of age who might be helpful and recommended I visit her. The woman stated she did not know my Grandmother Morgan, but there had been a family of Morgans who had lived next door to her for years but now they were living several miles away in Cherry Flats. I phoned those people, and they invited me over to visit.

This Morgan woman indicated she did not know my ancestor, Giles Morgan, but said, "I have a diary that belonged to my grandfather, and you may look at it. I have called my cousin, and she is bringing the Morgan Bible!" To my amazement and delight that diary contained the record of my ancestor, Giles Morgan, his parents and sisters and brothers. In it I came across the statement, "Giles is helping build the new home with his brother." The Bible record proved that we three have the same great-grandfather!

Additional searches took me to Towanda, Pennsylvania. There I was introduced to the courthouse records where I searched for

Morgan and Ballard wills. To my satisfaction I found a Herman Morgan will. The clerk then invited me into his office where he produced a very, very thick packet which contained various legal documents and a detailed description of the wealth and beauty of my Grandmother Morgan's home. There were statements by relatives revealing many positive situations and characteristics of the family.

Herman Morgan was from Blandford, Massachusetts. I became obsessed with straightening out Morgan lines. In Blandford the clerk was extremely rude to me, saying, "I can't be bothered today. Make another appointment." What a rebuff! I had traveled five hundred miles to see her. She added, "Anyway, the records were all burned. Why don't you see Mrs. . . , the past historian for Blandford." When I objected to her lack of interest, she slammed the door in my face. I was tired and very discouraged.

I drove down the road, and for some unknown reason stopped at a small white house. A friendly lady came to the door, and I asked if she knew Mrs. . . . I explained why I needed to see those records. Her husband called out, "I will call her," which he did, then said, "You will never find the place. She lives out in the country. I will show you the way." That evening at her home was one of the most fascinating I have ever spent in searching genealogy. The woman's three-hundred-year-old home was next door to the home and farm of Simon Morgan, father of Herman Morgan. It was like a walk into the past. She gave me all kinds of references and records and sent more later. After searching Vermont and Massachusetts, I found Simon Morgan buried in the state cemetery of Mansfield, Pennsylvania. Simon and his father were both Revolutionary War soldiers whose lines have now been documented for N.S.D.A.R. From the same clerk's proffered information, I documented the Morgan line to Miles Morgan of 1615, and I am pleased to state that the well-known J. P. Morgan also descends from this ancestor. The help I was given by so many people makes me feel as though someone had led me to them.

Two years before I began this long search for my Morgan family, I took an ocean cruise. On the ship I met a woman whose grandfather had done considerable research on the Ballard line. She gave me the name of a man I could consult in hopes of sharing their accumulated data. To my delight this resulted in extending my Ballard line back three generations. Many family members have supplied facts to aid my search for information. My ninety-two year old aunt gave me an obituary which dated back about thirty years. From this information I found relatives who never realized they had any living cousins on the Ballard line. I have now completed Ballard, Fox, Bowman and Morgan lines back to 1600.

For years I had wanted a photograph of my Grandfather Ballard as his cherished picture was lost in a flood. I borrowed one from a generous relative to make a copy. The owner eventually wanted it back, and it became an embarrassing situation as she continued to ask me for the original which I could not find. One day I put my hand on Joseph Ballard's Bible and said, "Joseph, you have got to help me find that picture." I walked over to the bookcase, reached in and pulled that original picture out of a travel magazine. My children said, "Mother, it is all right for you to talk to your ancestors, but please let us know when they talk back to you!"

Working on my genealogy has been an experience that has given me peace of mind and breadth of vision. I cannot explain it exactly, but it is as though arms of love have reached out to protect me as I have searched in many states. These travels have produced unexpected contacts in unusual places, unknown family connections and extensive records. These experiences have helped me grow and to know my family that I never knew before and for whom my heart had yearned.

ELEANOR RECTOR'S BEQUEATHAL

By Hartman Rector, Jr.

The most important gift I have ever received came from a total stranger. It happened this way.

In July 1979 I was assigned as a Managing Director of the Genealogical Department of The Church of Jesus Christ of Latter-day Saints. This department has a mission to provide leadership in turning the hearts of the children and fathers to one another in the process of building and strengthening eternal families; assist individuals and institutions to preserve precious records of mankind against disaster; record and preserve non-member and member family data and other official records, as well as records of temple ordinances; and provide resources, services and support to enable Church members to fulfill their divinely assigned responsibility to their kindred dead.

Therefore, among other activities, I became involved in promoting attendance to the second World Conference on Records scheduled to be held in Salt Lake City, Utah in August of 1980. The promotional activities required much travel and many speeches and extended efforts over an eight-month period informing interested persons about the unique advantages of the conference. One of the members of the Quorum of the Twelve Apostles, who was formerly an advisor to the Genealogical Department, upon hearing of my rather extensive endeavors, remarked to me, "Hartman, because of your efforts in behalf of this Genealogical Conference, the Lord will do something nice for you and your family." I did not attach any hopeful significance to this remark, but it did register in my memory as we always listen when the Lord's "annointed" speak.

In July of 1980 I received a letter from a recent convert to the Church, Pete Bogardus, introducing himself and telling me of a visit he had made to his parents' retirement home on one of the San Juan Islands in Puget Sound. It seems his parents had been retired about three years and had built a home on the island, Friday Harbor. They owned other property there, located next door to Ed (Lewis Edwin) and Eleanor (Johnson) Rector, who were both retired medical doctors, he from the U.S. Naval Service. Ed and Eleanor had become very interested in genealogy, so when they retired they spent twenty-six months traveling about the United States in a mobile home doing genealogical research on their family lines. They had *eleven volumes* of Rector family genealogical data on the library shelves of their home there on Friday Harbor Island. Pete Bogardus had seen these Rector volumes among others in Ed and Eleanor's collections. He wondered if I would be interested. He had read about me in a recent

Church publication and so he knew that I too was a convert to the Church who had been called as a General Authority with a current assignment in genealogy.

Of course, I *was* interested and immediately placed a call to him to find out more about these records which might include my people. In the letter he indicated that Eleanor was suffering from terminal cancer and probably would not live very long, so I must hurry if I wanted to see her astounding collection and discuss the Rector genealogy with her. As much as we wanted to see those records, my vacation time was gone and my weekends were scheduled with stake conferences and other assignments. My wife, Connie, and I prayerfully turned the situation over to the Lord.

As it turned out, the Church had scheduled the dedication of the Washington Temple in Bellevue, Washington, for the week of November 17, 1980. I was selected as one of the General Authorities to take part in the dedication! Therefore, I *would be* in the area to participate on November 20 and could possibly make a personal visit to the Rector home if Eleanor's condition would permit. Pete Bogardus felt that this was a feasible alternative to coming sooner, and in fact spoke to his parents about inviting me to spend the evening of the twentieth with them and introducing me to the Rectors on the twenty-first. It would be a tight schedule, for our group's return flight was also preplanned for the twenty-first.

I was scheduled to speak at the 1:30 p.m. temple dedicatory session which ended at 3:30 p.m. My wife, Connie, and I left immediately thereafter in a rented car for Anacortes, Washington, where we were to catch the ferry boat. We must make the Friday Harbor Ferry by 5:00 p.m. or wait until the next morning, but it was eighty miles away and there was a driving rainstorm! We made it with ten minutes to spare—parked the car and scurried aboard the ferry. It was a beautiful ride through the Puget Sound and the San Juan Islands, so named by the Spanish explorer who first visited the area. We arrived at 6:50 p.m. and were met by Pete Bogardus and his wife, Ramona. It was still raining but did show some signs of letting up.

The Bogarduses received us graciously, and we spent a most enjoyable evening with them and their friends. Friday morning we were greeted by a beautiful blue sky and bright sunshine. We went to the home of Ed and Eleanor Rector with the Senior Bogarduses and were warmly welcomed. As we visited together, Ed showed us his Navy memorabilia, which I especially enjoyed. Eleanor was a devoted genealogist and took great pride in showing us her extensive library. Although a medical doctor by profession, she had the most beautiful and legible handwritten records I have ever seen! I chuckle whenever I read them and think, she must have been a great disappointment to her medical professors because her prescriptions would actually be readable!

I explained to Eleanor that the Church had the facilities to film her vast finished collection of records. She was so very hopitable in spite of her illness and completely agreeable, even excited, to provide me *copies* of all her eleven-volume compilation of Rector data which was organized into large three-ringed binders. In fact, this fine Baptist lady said, "Now that I know the Mormon Church is interested in my research, what I have done will never be lost or wasted." She also expressed appredciation for the availability of the facilities of the genealogical library in Salt Lake City which she had used on occasion.

Eleanor's eleven large volumes of Rector research contained hundreds of pictures, documents, and other source materials. She was still working on these. She had also prepared five binders of pedigree and family group sheets extracted and copied from the original research. She gave them to Connie and me to take back to Salt Lake City to be microfilmed. Eleanor told us that all of the Rector volumes would be willed to me at her demise. Ed agreed wholeheartedly with every decision Eleanor made regarding the genealogy. As we sat by the large picture window, watching the boats sailing by, the Rectors served us delicious refreshments. It was a lovely, peaceful setting, and the Rectors were wonderful people who made us feel right at home.

In Salt Lake City, after the five volumes were filmed, they were sent to The Memorial Foundation of the Germanna Colonies in Virginia (of Culpeper County, Virginia), according to Eleanor and Ed's wishes.

Eleanor Johnson Rector died in December of 1981. Her husband survived her but soon after became disabled. A short time later we received in the mail a large carton which contained the eleven volumes of Rector genealogy. It was mailed to us by Eleanor's sister who was the executive of her will. Eleanor had bequeathed her original family collection to me as she had promised. All of these records have now been photographed and are available on microfilm in the Genealogical Library in Salt Lake City, Utah (and will ever be).

In our *previous* Rector researching, my wife and I had read a rare book in the San Francisco Sutro Library about the original John Jacob Rector, who came to Virginia in 1714 as an iron worker from Nassau-Siegen, Germany. There were many first-name similarities with my own family in Missouri. Therefore, I felt it was my line, but we had never been able to find the connection between the Rectors of Virginia and mine of Kentucky and Missouri, although I felt they probably followed the typical migration pattern from Virginia through the Cumberland Gap into Kentucky and then to Missouri.

I once paid $1500 to a genealogical research organization to link me with the descendants of John Jacob Rector of Virginia. They searched and provided me with much assorted information but never found the specific connection. Finally they said, "We feel this is your line." I said, "Feel! Hey, I have *felt* it for years, but that is not good enough. I want to see the *proof.*" I'm glad that in their honesty they did *not* prefabricate a *proof* in order to please me.

Eleanor and Ed Rector accumulated and compiled *many* records and in so doing found the "link." I was *not directly* related to John Jacob Rector but was a direct descendant from Johannes Richter or John Rector, the 1734 immigrant, who was "almost certainly" a *nephew* of Joh Jacob Rector, the 1714 immigrant. Our John came to America with a later group of Nassau-Siegen immigrants.*

In Eleanor's compilation there are in excess of 30,000 lineage-linked Rectors, whose records I was bequeathed. Surely the Lord *did* do something very nice for me and my family.

Germanna Records, #4 April 1963, page 79.

ROSA'S TREAT

By Rosa V. Lauritzen

I was born Maria del Rosario Vasquez in Coatza Coalcos, Vera Cruz, Mexico. The Spanish name of my town or village was Puerto Mexico, but according to an old Indian legend, it was renamed Coatza Coalcos, meaning 'God was there.'

My parents separated when I was very young, so I was raised by an aunt and uncle in Mexico City. I seldom saw my parents who lived some distance away. Their lives were very sad during those years. I was fortunate to have my "Uncle Father" Vincente and my "Aunt Mother" Josefina, whom I dearly loved. They were unable to have children of their own, so they lavished all their love and affection on me.

The religion of our family was a strong influence in my life, but I always had the feeling something was missing. One Sunday I was out horseback-riding and heard beautiful music. I rode closer. A small congregation was singing hymns. They were holding church in a small building. I joined them for the service and heard them speak of Christ. Also, a modern-day prophet and twelve apostles which was new to me. I felt at home and went again the following week and every week thereafter. I felt happy and at peace, especially when I learned that families can be together for eternity. I decided I would wait to marry until I found someone who felt as I did. My new faith strengthened and sustained me. My parents were disappointed but supported my decision to be baptized into the Church of Jesus Christ of Latter-day Saints.

I met my future husband, Roy Lauritzen, a member of my new faith. We fell in love, married and moved to America to begin life together. We married again in the Salt Lake Temple for time and all eternity. It was wonderful! Roy and I had four children: Sandra, Mary Ann, Roy Jr., and Rosey and were very busy with our family, employment and church activity.

When I heard about genealogy and temple work, I was thrilled, for we have many ancient temples in our land. The Lord's people have always built temples, even from Old Testament days. After my parents died, we accomplished their temple ordinance work so they could have the opportunity of being together always (if they chose to accept the vicarious work).

Sometimes Roy and I would take our children for a vacation to visit their Mexican grandparents and relatives. I located a few records of my father's and mother's families and several of my grandparents but did not have very much success. It seemed that either people were not interested, records were missing or letters went unanswered. Finally, I put the genealogy aside and concentrated on my other responsibilities. However, my heart continued to turn toward my Mexican relatives.

After my parents died, Roy and I were visiting my stepmother in my father's house (in Mexico). One afternoon I had a very beautiful experience. As I was resting by my sleeping children, I looked through the window and caught a glimpse of the handsome face of my deceased father! He had a very sweet expression of love in his eyes as he gazed proudly down on our little family. I glanced over at the children for only an instant, and when I looked back, he was gone. I felt he had come to let me know he had accepted the temple work and was very proud of me and of our family. At last, he was happy!

Time passed all too quickly, and our children were growing up. Our daughter, Sandra, married and began a family of her own. We moved to a new neighborhood. People were friendly and soon we felt right at home. One friend, an avid genealogist, offered to help me with my research, but I was just *too busy!*

One spring morning the phone rang and this friend was on the other end of the line. She had been trying all morning to reach me. I was surprised when she began, *"I'm late, Rosa, in reminding you to do your genealogy!"* She told me she had made a New Year's resolution to be a better neighbor and help me with my research, but I was always so busy. Then her resolution was put to the test! She went on:

"Early this morning I awoke remembering an unusual dream about you and your family. You were all standing in your large living room looking toward the front door as if waiting for something to happen. You had such a sweet spirit of love, Rosa. Only then did I realize that I was barefoot and in my flannel lavender-flowered nightgown! My goodness, I thought, I must have overslept. When I looked at my watch, it was *11:30* a.m.

"I hurriedly gathered up my clothing, but it was too late. When I looked through the front window, I saw two brethren from our church approaching. Rosa, you flung open the door and greeted them warmly. I felt embarrassed and not prepared, but no one seemed to notice. While they visited together, Roy Jr. extolled his mother's virtues and offered everyone a bite of something delicious she had made. 'Try it,' he encouraged. He walked over and offered the plate to me. I hesitated, so he handed me a taste of an unusual golden grain that had been sweetened and prepared in a special way. It was scrumptious!

"In the next scene I was (finally) dressed and standing with your family in a well-lighted storage room in your home. Boxes and barrels of food lined the walls. It was a pleasant place to be. Roy Jr. was nearby, so I quietly asked him for another bite of the delectable treat. He smiled, opened one of the large containers and said, 'See, there's plenty'! It was true. The barrel was full, near to overflowing. Roy reached in and handed some to me. The unusual grains were similar to wheat, golden brown on the outside, yet soft and pure white on the inside. They were sweetened with honey, yet each grain was smooth, separate and distinct from the other. (What *were* these unusual grains?) I somehow felt the intrinsic worth of each one. Rosa, you stood in the background, beaming all the while.

"When I awoke, I felt that the Lord was reminding me that it was indeed later than I realized, as shown by the 11:30 time on my watch. So, I called you. I knew I must hurry and make preparations to help with your genealogy. In the dream Roy Jr., the heir of your deceased father's family, was showing me that this work would be a real treat and very delicious when sweetened with love—and there was a whole barrelful to be done! I felt that each special grain represented a person with a golden skin on the outside and a pure spirit on the inside. Each one would be a beautiful addition to your family tree!" What an interesting dream, I thought! Especially since she had not known that one of my family's favorite dishes is cooked whole-grain wheat, sweetened with honey!

As our telephone conversation concluded, we set a day the

following week to go to the genealogical library. I felt that the Lord had given my neighbor a true dream, so I said, "Yes, it is time. We will go." I hurriedly hung up the phone so I would not be late for work.

At the library we were fortunate to encounter Lyman Platt, consultant over the Spanish records. "I was just leaving," he said. "You caught me at exactly the right time." After I explained some of my complicated situations of my parents and grandparents, he understood why I had shelved my genealogy for twenty years! I was counseled to begin again and not overlook even one name. Lyman showed me how to research and write for the Catholic records of the towns where my grandparents have lived. We studied many pages of a large atlas and also the history of several towns.

I began a search of the card file, but most of the records we needed had not yet been filmed. How discouraging! Back at the table we reviewed my records. The information had been difficult to accumulate. I carefully listed my father's first family with the three children in order of birth, then began on the next family. All too soon we came to a stopping point.

"What else shall we do?" was the next question. I recalled the night last summer when I dreamed of my uncle, Leoncio Vasquez, my father's brother. I have dreamed of him many times before, but this time he came to me around midnight, stood close by my bed and spoke to me in both Spanish and English (since my English is not so good). *"Get up and keep-a-goin' on your genealogy,"* he said. *"You're lazy!"*

Well, I couldn't take that lying down! I got out of bed, put on my robe and slippers and went downstairs. And there, right on top of my box of papers (although I had looked for them many times) were Leoncio's records. I felt he wanted his temple work done! Even after that I never did find time to work on his family. Now here I was at the library, and I had forgotten those papers again! Yet, for some reason, I reached into my flat, black leather folder. "Why here are Leoncio's papers! I *know* I did not put them there! We hugged each other and then began to fill out a family sheet for my uncle and his wife. I was ecstatic!

My friend then suggested, "Perhaps you should look in your

little case again." It was empty I was sure, but to please her, I did. Oh, I couldn't believe it! I found two more papers, a narrow-lined sheet with penciled notes and a small green one shaped like a Christmas ornament. They listed a few more names and places we could check in the file. Lyman Platt returned and found that one of the villages was actually listed under a completely different name. I hurriedly searched the file for the proper place, name and film number. It was almost closing time, so we finished the several family group sheets, ordered a film for the following week and hurried triumphantly out the door.

At home I prayerfully wrote several letters to relatives to obtain necessary bits of information. Then I unexpectedly discovered some important letters and records. Among my mementos were pictures of my handsome father dressed in military uniform, my smiling Uncle Leoncio, and my bearded aging grandfather, Nieves Davalos, who was 97 years old when he died.

The night after my friend and I had gone to the library, I had a wonderful dream. I was taken to meet many hundreds of my ancestors in village after village in Mexico. We were so happy to meet one another. We held hands, ran and jumped and danced together as in a giant fiesta. It was so wonderful, and I felt I was really there! When I awoke I asked my husband, "Are you really sure I was here all night?" He laughed and said, "Yes, but you made so much noise sleeping, it woke me up!"

The next day at work I was so weary. When my supervisor asked if I was sick, I told her I was just tired as I had been dancing all night. She looked puzzled so I explained my joyous experience to her, too. It is amazing to realize that my ancestors are so happy, knowing they are being remembered and their temple work will soon be done!

Some time later I had another experience concerning my Grandfather Davalos. I could not seem to get his records straight, and finally I threw up my hands in despair and cried, "Oh, Grandfather, why you do this to me? How am I *ever* going to find all your wives and children? You don't miss one second in this life!" That same night I saw my grandfather in a dream. With a twinkle in his eye and a mischievous grin, he chortled, *"Ho, ho, ho . . . you're cute!"* Now, how could I be mad at him? I think I cannot ever forget any of my ancestors. Each one is so special. So I must keep working to solve even the complicated problems. I am so thankful to the Lord for my wonderful family, and the help He is giving me in finding their difficult records.

I recall something very significant about the day my friend phoned telling of her dream. She had been "asleep" and not helping me. As she checked the time, it was *11:30* a.m. When she woke up, she had to phone several times to reach me. She shared her dream and set the date to begin my genealogy, Then I hurriedly hung up the phone so I would not be late for work. When I checked my watch, it was also exactly *11:30 a.m.*!

CONVINCING EVIDENCE
By Zdenka Kucera

As well as having a private practice as a genealogical researcher, I have also worked for the Genealogical Society in the cataloging department. When some of my patrons have had a special love for their ancestors and for their Father in Heaven, I have witnessed that they have been rewarded with special help.

One day a lady from Canada came to me and asked if I could help with her genealogy. She was sure that her Cook family had come from a little village, named Besco in Poland. (Even though the name of the village was misspelled, I was able to locate it on the map.) Since the name of Cook does not exist in Poland, I suggested that her ancestor had probably changed his name when coming to America. Many Slavic people do. She told me that she had exhausted all research possibilities in an effort to find out what his Polish name had been. "But," she said, "I will fast and pray about it."

For a few minutes I sat there trying to think of anything else she could do, then said, "Perhaps someone in the family has some old papers they consider insignificant. You might find something there to give you a clue." She promised to do what she could and left.

In about a month I received a letter from her telling me that as a result of fasting and prayer, she had received a strong impression to go visit a previously uncommunicative uncle. She tried to explain her genealogical problem to him, but he was not interested. Yet after a time he said, "There are some old letters and papers up in the attic in a shoe box. If you want to go through them, help yourself. I don't care about such things." Buried deep in the little box of miscellaneous triva, she found a paper on which was written: "If somebody ever will be interested in my name back in Poland, it was Kaczurowski, and I changed it to Cook." With this information, she was now able to search the records of the village of Besco. As a result, she found thousands of names of her ancestors—almost all of the inhabitants of the village were related to her in some way!

It seems that when my patrons come to a stopping point and have done all they can, if they care deeply enough about the work, answers will come almost miraculously. For example, a couple came to me two or three times to ask if I could help them find their ancestors from Czechoslovakia (formerly Austro-Hungarian Empire). Unfortunately, they did not know the locality and with nearly fifteen million inhabitants in this area, a search could not be undertaken without more information. When it seemed nothing could be done to find their families, they were both unhappy.

I don't know why, but during our third visit together I suddenly remembered the old picture album my grandmother had left us that had been in our family for a long time. I was covered in red velvet and had a gold title plate. Even though I had not seen it for many years, I could see it clearly in my mind. This gave me an idea, and I asked, "Please, don't you have any old picture albums at home?" "Oh, yes," they replied. "Nothing is written in them, however, and we don't know who the people in the pictures are." I asked, "Did you ever check the other side? Sometimes the place where the picture was taken is recorded on the back." When they told me the pictures were all glued to the pages of the album, I suggested that they at least remove the very old pictures and check them for clues.

Several days later they returned with a very exciting discovery! On the back of one of the pictures they found handwriting in a language they could not understand. The message had been written in an unschooled hand, without punctuation, and with all the words running together. Unscrambled it read, "Mehaly Hascak with his family from Zobrucneho." This place could not be located in the gazeteer. After some thought, I realized that the preposition "from" (which is "z" in Czech) had been placed in front of the place name. Obrucne was the correct name of the little village in Slovakia where this family originated. These folks were thrilled to be able to proceed with the research work and to learn more of their family heritage.

Indexing is very important. We must be sure that if the records are there, the patrons can find a reference to them in the card file. There are times I have felt a very strong impression to go back and recheck my work. Then I have found I had missed something very important. I have often thought of all the people in those records who would not have been found if I had not followed those promptings. At times like these I have a feeling that we are being helped by unseen persons who care very much about this work.

While in cataloguing I had another experience where I was able to help a lady who once lived in Russia with her family. When she was a young girl, her leg was amputated. Later she came to the United States with her parents, married, and had children. She wanted me to help her find her ancestors but she had very little information. The name of her village, Dabrowa, was very common in Poland. There were perhaps three hundred villages by that name! (This problem came about because this part of Poland had once belonged to Russia, then had been returned once more to Poland.)

I asked my patron for an identifying name of a place near her village, for the common German name could not be located. Afterwards, I thought a lot about this sweet lady who was not well and not expected to live long. She wanted very much to find the records of her people.

One day while checking some microfilm records for cataloging , I came across a parish with a completely different name than the ones she had given me. Yet, I noticed the same surname of this little lady. At first I passed it by because the name was so common that it would have been a miracle to find her family there. Yet something just wouldn't let me go further, so I turned back and, sure enough, there was her family! Even the name of the village was there, a village so small that it belonged to another parish where the records were kept. The odds against *ever* finding that village were enormous. Except for the inner promptings I received, I am sure I never could have found it.

Some may try to explain away these miracles, but it seems to me that, especially when taken all together, they are convincing evidence that the Spirit of the Lord is guiding this work. It is up to each of us to put ourselves in tune with that Spirit and listen. Direction will come.

I LOVE MY CHILDREN
By Rose Hinton

As a genealogist of my Scott family, I was concerned that in three years in that position I had found nothing on the direct lines of Joshua Scott and Nancy Keen. Nor had anyone else been successful in the last seventy-four years. It was early spring, and I began praying with intensity for help in finding something before the family reunion the following summer.

I had a dream one morning, just before waking. I dreamed I had begun building a house but had only completed the foundation. I left the house at that stage and went to church one Sunday; when I came back, there stood a mansion, completely built. Not only that but the yard was beautifully landscaped with a low wall around it. Even in my dream I knew that only the Lord could have built it in such a short time. I awoke knowing without any doubt that this dream referred to my Scott genealogy.

About that time I became strongly impressed with the name Syrach Titus, and I thought about it continuously. This was a name I had seen in the early Dutch records of New York where I had done research for the other side of my family. I knew it had nothing to do with the Scotts. However, as the impression persisted, I began making a Titus file. Whenever I found a Titus name, I recorded it and put it in that file. I felt that I didn't have time to concentrate on it, because I had to work on the Scott family lines for the reunion.

The reunion came and went without my having anything to add to our pedigree. Following the reunion, I decided that the first thing I must do was to see why the name Syrach Titus was impressing me so much. In the New York records, I found the first of the line in this country, a Titus Syrachs who had a son, Syrach Titus, which followed the patronymic system. Each generation after him had a son of this latter name.

I followed the family for two or three generations and discovered that a Syrach Titus moved over into Bucks County, Pennsylvania, where my Scott people were. There was a Dutch church record in Bensalem, Bucks County, where I had found a Nancy Keen's christening; but it was several years earlier than the date I had for Nancy's birth, so I dismissed it.

Since Syrach Titus was Dutch, this Dutch church seemed the logical place to look for him. As I went through the church record again, I was gratified to find descendants of many of my father's people from New York and New Jersey. Then I came upon an entry of a christening of a Syrach Titus! His wife's name was Annatie Strickler. This I immediately associated with the christening of the Nancy Keen I mentioned, because her mother was Marya Strickler.

At that moment it was made known to me that this was my family! I spent three months continuing the search to complete this family unit and trace its ancestry. During that time I had a glorious feeling with me. I felt a guiding hand in everything I did; and inspiration in the sources I searched. I was shown how to evaluate them. Ultimately, I had one line to the earliest Swedes of Pennsylvania, and another to the earliest Dutch of New York.

Still, it seemed that there was something more about Syrach Titus that I needed to know. In the Titus file where I had put bits and pieces of information were two childrens' christening records from a New York Dutch church. I felt compelled to record these names—an extreme pressure, in fact—although I did not know who they were. As I did so, I felt an intense sense of relief.

One day I picked up an old archive family record of Teunis Nyssen, one of my father's direct lines. Teunis was an early Dutch immigrant of New York. I saw with surprise that the spouse of Jannetje Teunis, one of his daughters, was Titus Syrachs, the first of the Titus line mentioned above! On a later archive record for Teunis Nyssen, and on all the other sources I had seen, she had been listed with another husband. The archive record showing her as a mother, indicated she was married to Jan Hansen Bergen.

Shortly after this, I copied the complete old Dutch church registers of Flatbush and Brooklyn as I was related to many people in them. That night after going to bed I began thinking of the name of Syrach Titus and became increasingly wide awake. At last I got out of bed, picked up my case with the New York Dutch church records in it and tiptoed into the study. I began reading those two records and discovered from the christenings of Titus Syrach's children and the witnesses that he was the husband of Jannetje Teunis (Nyssen). The wife of Jan Hansen Bergen was Jannetje Teunis (Coevert). This mistake had easily been made because only the patronymic of Teunis had been used by both Jannetjes, and the records had been confused.

As this realization came to me, my soul filled to overflowing with joy. I felt the presence of Titus Syrachs, and his joy at my discovery. For a long time it seemed that we communed, not in words, but in emotion. Finally I asked, "What would you say to me?" The answer flowed into my mind, bringing tears to my eyes, "I love my children."

IVY, IT'S MY TURN

By Ivy L. Watson Larsen

"Ivy, it's my turn." These are the words I heard in August of 1962 when my father, George M. Larsen, spoke to me, spirit to spirit. On that day I was at home working on genealogy in my living room. I had just finished the research for one of my patrons. I started to reach for another client's file when I heard his voice. I said to myself, "What does my father want me to do? Where does he want me to work?" He had passed away only six months earlier. I thought about my promise to him.

Several years before, my father had offered to pay my tuition for a series of university classes on Danish genealogy if I would do his Danish research. As he lived far from the library and needed my assistance, I promised to help him. I enrolled in the university and there studied historical and genealogical records, phonetics, grammar and vocabulary. I was also taught customs and trends, census and probate records, and military levying rolls, all of which helped me find and accurately identify complete families.

Learning to read and write the Gothic script was great fun! I practiced writing in Gothic by copying paragraphs from newspapers and magazines then exchanging with friends and reading what they had written. Then I was able to read the Danish parish registers. My studies were so rewarding I could not leave them alone. I kept searching and reading, and the more I practiced the easier the task became. At length, I completed the courses and received my certificate. I mentioned to my husband, Glenn J. Watson, that if anything ever happened to him, I would have a way to support my children. At the time, I did not realize how soon this would be. A short time later, after a period of illness, my father died. I did not forget my promise to him.

I had recently turned in several of my father's family group sheets to the library to be checked and was anxiously waiting for their return to see what more I needed to do. They had not arrived. I desired so very much to have those sheets on his Danish ancestry. I was trying to decide what to do when the mailman came and left the very records I was waiting for.

I immediately recognized the hand of the Lord in this and felt sure that there was something within these sheets that my father wanted me to follow up. As I laid them out on the table and examined them, I felt exceedingly happy. I noticed on one of the sheets, concerning my direct pedigree line, that the one who had checked my records had added the day, month, and year of birth but not the father of my fifth great-grandfather. I had entered only an "about" year of birth for him. I knew that in a parish register when a full birth date is given, that at least the father's name is recorded in the entry. If the checker had the birth information, why not the father's name? Why had this information been left out? If I had that name, my pedigree line would be extended another generation. The feeling came over me that this was where my father wanted me to work.

I gathered up the sheets and went to the genealogical library. I made an appointment to see the girl who had checked my records and asked her about the family group sheet in question. She indicated she did not have access to the information in her department. She answered, "I would have written in the name if it had been on the card." She went back into the files, pulled the card and showed it to me. The day, month, and year of birth was entered, but not the father's name.

I thanked her and went downstairs to get a reading machine. I knew Father wanted me to work on the next generation back. This would put me back into the middle 1600s in the Danish records. In those days it was necessary to fill out a form to receive a film, which I did. I was so excited I could hardly wait for the film to come. When it arrived, I turned to the birth entry of my ancestor to find his father's name. Then I planned on searching for his brothers and sisters and other descendants.

To my dismay this part of the record was written in an unfamiliar old-style Gothic script. Ordinarily, I could decipher the Gothic script in the Danish records, but this record I could not read. I was able to read the father's name and also see other entries pertaining to this family, but I knew I could not gather all of the family together and their descendants without making mistakes. I had to read the record! I had to read the old-style Gothic script! I could have cried, and tears did come. I picked up my things and went home.

That night I prayed to my Heavenly Father for help. I told him about my father coming to me and wanting my help. I explained how I felt about this part of the pedigree line being what my father wanted me to work on and how I couldn't read it. I pleaded with him for his help and direction in understanding the script.

Before my father died he told me that he had always wanted to teach the gospel to his people in their native tongue, but he had not had the opportunity to do so. My father was a missionary for his church but never had the opportunity to go to Denmark where his father was born. Then a short time later he died. I felt strongly that my father was now fulfilling his lifelong dream in the spirit world. I also felt that he had come to encourage me to continue to research our family and organize the records in an acceptable way. I told my Father in Heaven how I felt and asked for his help. Then I retired for the night.

The next morning I again prayed fervently for his assistance. I went to the library and again sat down at a reader and turned to the page on the film I wanted to read. With a prayer in my heart I studied that record. I had casually looked at my watch when I started. I studied and concentrated on that old Gothic script and together with the Gothic I already knew, the Lord helped me to understand it. It was as if he gave me the knowledge and planted it into my mind. I was reading it, and I knew I was doing it right! and only fifteen minutes had passed!

My spirits soared as I realized that the record was full of my father's people and mine. Over the next few weeks whenever I was able to go to the library, I continued to work on this record. I had a husband and a family of children in school, and I could not devote my whole time to research work. I was so determined to finish the records of my father's family, however, that I spent every available hour that I could find in preparing these records.

Then unexpectedly, my husband passed away with a heart attack. It was such a shock. With one son married, two sons in the mission field, and two sons and a daughter attending school, it seemed such a tragedy. Our youngest son was eight year old, not quite nine.

For six weeks I did not enter the library; six weeks of taking care of business matters and sinking deeper into feeling sorry for myself. Then my father spoke to me again saying, "Ivy, you have rested long enough. It's time to get busy." I knew what my father meant. I gathered up my records and went back to the library. The knowledge that the Lord had given me of the old-style Gothic script was still with me, and I could read the records. With all the time I could afford away from my family during school hours, I continued to gather my father's records and organize them into families.

By the time January arrived I had found over 350 names! a whole congregation of people! I was so happy, and I felt that my father was happy, too. I was so thankful. With the help of the Lord I had been able to assist him in preparing the records of a congregation of people on the other side. It was a joyous experience!

From then on genealogy became my life's work. I took on extra work for other people to support my family. In the past few years I have been able to use my knowledge of languages in a new, yet related field. I have had the opportunity to learn and extract the records of Denmark, Norway, Sweden and Iceland. I am exceedingly happy to be able to do my part in this great work. I have found that humility, sincere prayer and a refusal to give up are the keys to successful research work. The many spiritual experiences I have had in this endeavor have greatly strengthened my testimony to where I know, beyond a shadow of a doubt, that this is the work of the Lord.

RENDEZVOUS WITH DESTINY
OF MITSUTAKA SHIGENOBU

By Diane L. Deputy

It was Saturday, July 23, 1977. As I boarded the train in Montreux, Switzerland I looked about for the proper seat for this was to be no ordinary journey. I had prayed each day and had been impressed to "return to Interlaken, *not* on Friday but on Saturday (in time for church on Sunday?)." Now, I was wondering *why*. When I spied a congenial family facing each other on double seats, I took a place as close as possible, across the aisle. They would be good traveling companions, I surmised. We exchanged a few pleasantries until a quiet voice within told me to "find another place!"

I moved ahead to the next car, looked about, then felt drawn to an empty seat on the right. I sat down just as the train lurched forward to begin its journey. No one else came in. (Perhaps I was meant to spend the time alone.) The train began its ascent up the hills toward the mountains. I relaxed, intent on the beautiful view of the Castle Chateau de Chillon, outlined against Lake Geneva with its surrounding picturesque landscape. Soon we sped by the station of Montbovan.

My thoughts were interrupted by a pleasantly modulated voice, "May-I-sit-here-please?" A young Japanese man who spoke halting English motioned to the vacant seat across from mine.

"Yes," I assured him, "you are welcome."

The young man nodded politely in assent, then turned and walked back down the aisle. A few moments later he returned weighed down with two large mountaineer backpacks, poles and other gear of a different kind than I had seen before. He saw my questioning expression and explained, "I go-climb-mountain." Since I knew there was a reason for my taking this particular train, I wondered why we were meeting. Surely our lives were worlds apart.

After his luggage was in order, he sat down opposite me and continued. "My name-Mitsutaka Shigenobu" (an honored name I could sense). "From Japan, and you?" I introduced myself as from America.

I sorry—I no speak English-good." Since I spoke no Japanese at all, I prayed for understanding for us both. "You-only person I talk to-all way from Japan," he volunteered. "All my life-I love-climb. I-great-desire to climb-great Eiger-in Swiss. I think-live all-life-for this time." The light of a great dream come true shone in his eyes.

"Do you work or go to school, in Japan?" I spoke slowly so he could understand.

"I go-school-and learn—very important."

"Have you family at home?"

The young man nodded, "Old mother-and-love-sister's family live-Niimi City, Okayama-ken. I-great love-for them. In Japan, children taught-respect for-parents and family. I love-father also-but he die." His voice trailed off.

The train stopped at Gestaad, interrupting our thoughts, then moved on.

"Do you believe you will see your father again in the next life?"

"I do not know-but I believe so." He gazed off into the distance as if searching for that knowledge. "How does one know what true religion? I see-much truth-everywhere. My family-belongs to-some-Shinto religion. But I-study many-religions and learn-many things. Are you-Christian?" he asked.

I nodded yes. "And if you will pray for truth, it will be given for you to follow." He paused and with a downward glance said, "I love honored father-very much. I hope-see-him-again."

Somehow I was able to perceive the deepest feelings of the young man before me. He grieved for his father. I felt a desire to help him understand the great yearning of his own soul for eternal life. I prayed for soft words of comfort, but instead was given strong words of depth and meaning. *"You will,"* I assured him. *"You will be with your father and your ancestors.* They are proud of you and love you very much! One day, you will be together again."

He smiled and nodded, "That is good."

Mitsutaka suddenly stood up and said no more but reached into his pack. He took out a small white packet. "I-gift-for you," he said modestly. "It is-small." I accepted the gracious gift in the manner it was given. Inside the white wrapping was a lovely gold-brocade "Komono Ire," a special little drawstring bag adorned with Oriental designs. I was pleased and thanked Mitsutaka. He smiled.

We rode in silence for a time. As we passed occasional villages set against the mountains, I continued to pray for direction. At Zweisimmen the train stopped, and a few passengers boarded or alighted. Our journey continued. . . .

"And what of your family records? The records of your ancestors?" He looked puzzled. I remembered the only Japanese word I knew, "the Kakocho!"

"Oh yes,-I-understand. Yes, very-important! But they are far away. My sister has Kakocho-at her home."

"You came a long way to climb a mountain, all the way to Switzerland! Are not the records of your family more important?"

He smiled, "Yes, that-is-true. I *will*-find-Kakocho,-family records of my ancestors."

"My friend in America and I did a book together. Many beautiful stories. One is Japanese about Kakocho. If you would like to read it, I will send it to you."

"Oh yes, I like-very much."

DIANE L. DEPUTY

"Tell me, if a father dies, does the son inherit or receive the family Kakocho?"

"Yes,-you-are-correct. I am to keep-for-family and when I marry-for-children." Mitsutaka looked very thoughtful.

The train stopped at Spiez just as the sun was departing. We changed trains, and the young man said, "Our time-almost gone. Today-pleasant. Let us-supper-together before day over." The reflection of the setting sun on the lake seemed only a continuation of the brightness of our day. Somehow in our moments together we had captured something as precious as fine crystal.

We stepped off the train at Interlaken, walked to one of the outdoor cafes and found a table. All too soon our simple meal was over. For some reason I could hardly bear to see Mitsutaka leave, and he seemed to feel the same. (Such a beautiful person of deep intellect and noble character.)

Perhaps he would not mind my asking, "Would you like to go to church with me tomorrow, Mitsutaka?" He hesitated, then glanced up at the majestic Alps. The fading sun's "alpine glow" of gold, rose and crimson seemed to warm those three great peaks; the Eiger, the Jungfrau, and the Monch, beckoning him on.

Mitsutaka answered, "No, I cannot go-church tomorrow, but maybe *next* time. . . . I go-to-climb a mountain!"

"Well, then, goodbye, Mitsutaka . . . goodbye." I waved. "And remember the Kakocho!"

"I will!" he cried as he also waved and moved away into the crowd. Once more he turned back and smiled. I returned his smile and whispered, "Remember!" A nod, and Mitsutaka Shigenobu was gone.

After returning to America, I sent the promised letter and book to my young Japanese friend. I looked forward to hearing about his Alpine adventures. At home in my living room, I sat down to rest a moment. Suddenly, nostalgic memories of Switzerland flowed over me. I felt such a deep longing for the beautiful homeland of my ancestors. Again I remembered the journey from Montreux to Interlaken and my friendship with Mitsutaka Shigenobu. Our meeting seemed so recent, as if it happened only yesterday. Once again I felt the sweetness of our friendship.

Then the postman came, interrupting my reverie. I hurried out to the box and reached for the mail. On the top lay a blue air-mail letter postmarked Japan! I quickly tore open the envelope, took out the letter and began to read:

No. _____

28th. march., 1978

Dear Mrs. Diane Deputy

It is the first time to write you. I'm the late Mitsutaka Shigenobu's elder sister. My only one brother, Mitsutaka was dead on his way in climbing up Eiger – West – Wall in Swiss. It happened in July the 27th. 1977. He called up me to start for Europe on the 2nd of July in 1977, at Japan time. He was supposed to come back to Tokyo on the 5th of August. But he has never come back. A few days later we heard about the bad news that he must have met with an accident — by foreign telegram from Ambassador in Swiss, because his sub-bag had been found by a German Alpinist and he told the policemen that it had been left on the snow in the west wall of Eiger, he also looked the marks of some avalanche.

We, old mother and my husband and I, started for Swiss right away, although we were afraid that it may be impossible to find anything buried under the snowslide. While applying to the police for a search, we had been praying for his safety. We had been praying on the airplane for Europe, and in the train for Swiss from France, and everywhere.

But we had got the worst news that his body had been found under the snow on just a night (on the 14th in August) when we had arrived at the hotel in Junore. My mother said with tear that his soul knew she had come to meet him. Next on the 15th of August, we held a short funeral in a small church in Lauterbrunnen, looking over beautiful mountains just like a picture.

By the way I found a post picture card (Kleine Scheidegg, the Grindelwalde, written by him for me, it was in the main bag left at Hotel in (Kline shaiguck). He had written it at Hotel in Interlaken. He said in it that he had met a kind American lady on the train, luckily he had made friends with her, and he had enjoyed to speaking with her in English so much, she said she would send her book. After that, back to Tokyo, on picking up his lodgings. I found an air-mail for him with the second of August stamp. I guessed that you had written that letter for him.

I'm very sorry that we almost forgot to write you. Thank you very much for your kind letter to my love brother. If he had been alive, how he would have been delighted to get your letter, and he would sure have sent you a letter or anything like that at once. We heard that during last summer, all over the Europe Alps, more than three hundred young people had met with accidents. It had been the worst weather in those hundred years.

I loved him, and he was very kind and good young man. We missed him so much. We wonder why he had climbed up that dangerous mountain by himself, because he was thought a sort of man of caution. Nobody knows that reason why. Maybe that most beautiful Dead-Man's mountain had charmed him.

Would you like to make friends with me for him? I want you to tell me about that day when you met him, and how he was. I'll write you about me and my family in next letter.

Sincerely Mrs. Reiko Mikami.

コクヨ ショ-10 (45×23)

135

By now the tears were streaming down my cheeks. Yes, Keiko, I will be your friend. Goodbye, Mitsutaka Shigenobu. We will meet again one day! Remember the Kokocho!